Caroline ——

Wild at Heart:
The Films of Nettie Wild

*You are a great
nurse & a great
pal in creating
art & revolution X*

Nettie

Wild at Heart:
The Films of Nettie Wild

ESSAY BY MARK HARRIS

INTERVIEW BY CLAUDIA MEDINA

PACIFIC CINÉMATHÈQUE MONOGRAPH SERIES
NUMBER TWO

24 per second
THE ANVIL FILM SERIES

Copyright © 2009 Pacific Cinémathèque Pacifique Society

Anvil Press Publishers Inc.
P.O. Box 3008, Main Post Office
Vancouver, B.C. V6B 3X5 CANADA
www.anvilpress.com

Library and Archives Canada Cataloguing in Publication
Harris, Mark
    Wild at heart : the films of Nettie Wild / Mark Harris ; interview by
Claudia Medina ; series editor: Brian Ganter.

(Pacific cinémathèque monograph series ; 2)
Includes bibliographical references.
ISBN 978-1-897535-03-5

    1. Wild, Nettie--Criticism and interpretation. 2. Wild, Nettie--Interviews.
I. Medina , Claudia, 1971- II. Title. III. Series: Pacific cinematheque monograph series ; 2

PN1998.3.W55H37 2009   791.4302'3092   C2009-904300-9

Printed and bound in Canada
Cover design: Mutasis Creative
Interior design: Heimat House
Anvil Film Series, *24 per second*, #2

Cover images: Top, Jo Jo Sescon; bottom, Elaine Briere
Photo of Nettie on horse by Robin Bain

Represented in Canada by the Literary Press Group
Distributed by the University of Toronto Press

Canadian   Patrimoine
Heritage   canadien

    The publisher gratefully acknowledges the financial assistance of the Canada Council for the Arts, the Book Publishing Industry Development Program (BPIDP), and the Province of British Columbia through the B.C. Arts Council and the Book Publishing Tax Credit.

CONTENTS

Preface

THE PACIFIC CINÉMATHÈQUE MONOGRAPH SERIES

Western Canadian cinema has been and continues to be one of the most geographically and artistically expansive, distinctive, and dynamic zones, both within the cultural borders of Canada and within the cinematic traditions of North American cinema. Yet it also remains, with a few exceptions, one of the most under-analyzed and underrepresented areas in both mainstream film studies and independent film criticism. The NFB documentary traditions that were forged in Ottawa, following on the heels of John Grierson and the post-1960s Québécois regional cinema led by Denys Arcand and Claude Jutra, have received their well-deserved critical dues. For too long now Western Canadian filmmaking practice has been simplistically categorized, to use the global vernacular, as a spin-off of "Hollywood North." A place for exploring and acknowledging the spectrum of contributions and innovations of Western Canadian filmmakers, videomakers, and fringe media artists is therefore long overdue.

The Pacific Cinémathèque Monograph Series emerged out of this somewhat shadowy status of Western Canadian cinema within the field of film studies in particular and in the world of film appreciation in general. The subject of this series is the wide range of film-, video and media-makers that have made significant contributions to either defining, expanding, or subverting the boundaries of Western Canadian cinema—from fringe to mainstream and back again—over the last fifty years. The series is overseen by the Education Department of the Pacific Cinémathèque. It builds on the success of Pacific Cinémathèque's Film Study Guide Series, and expands the audience of these popular guides by targeting film- and video-makers, film aficionados, undergraduate university students, and educators.

Each volume of the series will address an individual film- or media-maker and will consists of four different sections:

(i) A critical essay introduces the reader to the regional, sociological, and artistic influences of the filmmaker—establishing both a historical and an environmental context for their body of work.

(ii) An extensive interview provides a thorough examination of the themes and mechanics behind the narrative and stylistic sensibilities of the interviewee—providing an in-depth exploration of the unique traits of the artist.

(iii) A detailed filmography is included as a reference guide to the artist's body of work.

(iv) A working bibliography situates the films and the influence of the filmmakers in a network of references assembled from a variety of sources: encyclopedias of cinema, essays, books, journals, and magazines.

About the Project Supporters

Pacific Cinémathèque

Vancouver's Pacific Cinémathèque Pacifique is a not-for-profit society dedicated to fostering an understanding of film and moving images. Since 1972, the Cinémathèque's theatre and Education Department have been providing media education resources and materials to public schools across Canada. Through exhibitions, film tours, educational services, and film-related resources, Pacific Cinémathèque fosters critical media literacy and advances cinema as an art and as a vital means of communication in British Columbia and Canada.

AV Preservation Trust & Canadian Heritage

For the first volumes of the Monograph series, Pacific Cinémathèque has partnered with the AV Preservation Trust of Canada. The AV Preservation Trust is a charitable non-profit organization dedicated to promoting the preservation of Canada's audio-visual heritage, and to facilitating access to and usage of regional and national collections through partnerships with members of the audio-visual community. It is dedicated to increasing Canadians' awareness of their rich and distinctive heritage in moving images and sound. Working in collaboration with both public and private sectors, the AV Trust conducts a variety of programs designed to help tomorrow's generations see and hear the work of yesterday's and today's audiovisual creators.

This project was also made possible by funding provided through the Heritage Policy Branch of the Department of Canadian Heritage.

Acknowledgements

This Monograph volume is the result of the collaboration and input of a multitude of supporters and advisors who helped to guide the development and execution of the project. Appreciation goes out to all of the various dedicated hands and minds that made these volumes possible.

Special appreciation and recognition goes out to the following persons: Liz Schulze, Education Manager, Pacific Cinémathèque; Sally Stubbs, former Education Director, Pacific Cinémathèque; Dr. Stuart Poyntz, former Education Director, Pacific Cinémathèque; Jim Sinclair, Executive Director, Pacific Cinémathèque; Analee Weinberger, former Education Director, Pacific Cinémathèque; Colin Browne, filmmaker, writer and Professor, Contemporary Arts, Simon Fraser University; Caroline Coutts, Festival Director, Moving Pictures: Canadian Films on Tour; Zoë Druick, Assistant Professor, School of Communication, Simon Fraser University; Kelly Friesen, AV Preservation Trust; Marc Glassman, Editor, *POV*; Danielle Currie, Vancouver Art Gallery; Brian Kaufman, Anvil Press, and Steve Chow, Communications Manager, Pacific Cinémathèque.

In addition, special thanks for a variety of contributions are due to the following persons: Amber Rowell, Betty Lou Phillips, Vladimir Lubin, Natalie Clager, and Betsy Carson. The editor would like to thank Maryam Nabavi and Justin Page, whose unwittingly well-timed invitation to Saturna Island provided this editor with a pleasant working retreat to hammer out some of the final revisions on this volume. His thanks also to Stephanie Skourtes and Matteo Skourtes-Ganter for their unique and irreplaceable support. Claudia Medina and Mark Harris, the producers of this volume not only contributed their work, their creativity, and their intelligence but often generated materials and revisions under tight deadlines. Above all, the

Cinémathèque would like to extend its gratitude to Nettie Wild. Nettie not only donated many of the images for the volume from her private archives, but she also deserves high praise for the amount of careful checking, thoughtful review, and the relentless (in the best sense of that word!) critical reflection and creative input she has generously offered throughout this volume's publication process. Finally, we happily acknowledge that, throughout the development of this series, the Pacific Cinémathèque has relied on the resources of the Toronto Film Reference Library, the Ontario Cinémathèque, and the Vancouver Art Gallery.

—Brian Ganter, Editor,
on behalf of the Pacific Cinémathèque Education Department
Vancouver, BC, October 2009

Introduction

Ever since John Flaherty shot the first non-fiction feature film, *Nanook of the North* (1922), in Canada's Hudson Bay region and the socialist-minded John Grierson coined the phrase "documentary" before going on to found the National Film Board (NFB) in 1939, documentary has often been called Canada's 'national genre.' Its past and influence within the NFB have served as equal part inspiration and burden to later generations of independent filmmakers. Yet the frequency with which independent Canadian filmmakers have moved back and forth between fiction and non-fiction filmmaking—a relatively unique trait when compared to U.S. film culture where a more rigid division of labour prevails between the two—is strong evidence that, in this case at least, each form has benefited from the growth and the successes of the other.

Needless to say, the documentary genre has extended far, far beyond the old NFB in-house "style." The works of Michel Brault, Allan King, Alanis Obomsawin, Anne Wheeler, Catherine Annau, and Bonnie Sherr Klein, are only a few cases in point. Even more recently, the rise of the so-called "new political documentary" has further helped to expand and reenergize the ranks of a new wave of practicing documentarists. Led by Mark Achbar (*The Corporation*), Jennifer Baichwal (*Manufactured Landscapes*, *Payback*), and André-Line Beauparlant (*Trois Princesses pour Roland*), Canadian documentary has found itself reenergized and rediscovered by audiences eagerly seeking out new voices, new forms of public engagement, new approaches, new answers and, often, new questions.

No retelling of this history could possibly pass over the central role and the influence that Nettie Wild has had in the life of documentary filmmaking. Her commitment to the craft and to the value of independent filmmaking—from the first creative and collaborative moment to the final distribution of the end product—makes her an obvious choice to help launch this Monograph series.

Nettie Barry Canada Wild's wide-ranging career in the communicative and performing arts began in Vancouver well before she ever picked up a camera. The child of a journalist and an opera singer, she found herself working in the city's fringe theatre circles. Shortly before working as a CBC radio journalist she made her first forays into film, voicing the NFB shorts *Distant Islands* (1981) and *Gifted Kids* (1984) and recording sound for *Time to Rise* (1981). Her first self-driven film venture, *Right To Fight* (1982), a mix of musical and documentary, had its genesis in a live theatre production, *Buy Buy Vancouver*, which she co-wrote and co-produced as part of the Headlines Theatre collective.

Right to Fight yielded handfuls of awards and acclaim, but it was her 1988 feature documentary, *A Rustling of Leaves: Inside the Philippine Revolution,* that put her on the world cinema and documentary map. Wild's debut feature won the People's Choice Award at the 1988 Berlin Film Festival (Forum of New Cinema) and the Prix du Public at the NFB's Salute to the Documentary. Filmed in the wake of the overthrow of the Marcos dictatorship, *A Rustling of Leaves* confronted Wild with a rollercoaster ride of funding and insurance; a location replete with threats to life and health that often left her short of crew; subjects sometimes reluctant to be filmed; and a clash between progressive political militancy and the ethics of filming the execution of a young man charged with crimes against the movement. Yet it also set Wild off on a prolific filmmaking career that would continue its great leap forward across the decades.

Her next film, *Blockade: It's About the Land and Who Controls It* (1993), stands as an engaging and intimate portrait of a contest between the land claims of the Gitksan and Wet'suwet'en first nations and the white settler community's claims on logging rights that divides a community in Northwestern British Columbia. Broadly keeping to the subject of land rights, her next film, *A Place Called Chiapas* (1998), took her to the Zapatista camps and communities of southern Mexico. While the charismatic postmodern Marxist Subcommandante Marcos is often cited as the visual centerpiece of that movement and the film, the real focus of the film is the movement itself and its repeated clashes with both landowners and the right-wing military. The film struck a popular chord among filmgoers, premiering at the prestigious Berlin International Film Festival, and then returning to North America to capture the International Documentary Association's Award for Best Documentary. It went on that year to receive the Genie for Best Feature Documentary in Canada.

The latest phase of Wild's recent work has brought her back to the city streets at the very core of her home province, Vancouver's Downtown Eastside. The Downtown Eastside has become a legal, cultural, and especially political battleground in the past decades, most notably around the recently successful effort to establish North America's first and only safe injection site. In the tradition of other Vancouver-set portraits of non-mainstream urban life—most notably Alan King's *Skid Row* (1956) and Janis Cole and Holly Dale's *Hookers on Davie* (1984)—Wild's *FIX: The Story of An Addicted City* follows protagonists on both sides of the heated debate. In 2007, Wild explored new media with her latest endeavour, the controversial, interactive DVD, *Bevel Up: Drugs, Users and Outreach Nursing*. Developed in collaboration with a team of street nurses form the BC Centre for Disease Control, *Bevel Up* has played to sold-out audiences in Vancouver and Toronto. Distributed to health care professionals and community groups in Canada and internationally, it yielded numerous awards including a 2008 American Academy of Nursing Media Award. As an unofficial companion piece to *FIX*, *Bevel Up* functions both as a tutorial for, and a record of, practicing street nurses: a practical guide for those interacting with and treating people who use drugs.

Despite what might appear at first glance, as a verite or even social realist tone in her films, as Claudia Medina discovers in her interview in this volume, Wild still insists upon the appeal and the structure of dramatic story-driven editing, not at all typical for a documentary filmmaker. One need not look hard to find the patient development of character, the incremental build-up of dramatic incidents, or even attention to the nuances of romantic involvement in Wild's most seemingly hard-nosed political documentaries. The obvious care with which she selects editors and the weight she clearly places on character and story in her films are the first clues to her enduring dramatic sympathies. Yet another is the style of narration in her films. Here she frequently opts for the intimate "internal focalization" more typical of dramatic fiction—narrating only in terms of what the characters of the film already think, see, and know—rather than the distanced omniscient "external" narrative focalization of conventional documentary.

In his essay, Mark Harris provides us with an incisive and refreshing take on the broader scope of the films that make up Wild's *oeuvre*. Yet looking beyond the films themselves, Wild demonstrates an equally unbounded energy and creativity in the *distribution* of her work. Today the gaze of many independent filmmakers has turned to online distribution methods, often in the shorter formats that new media tends to embrace. Still, Wild attributes the traction gained by her four feature films (excepting *Bevel Up*) to the fact that they were distributed theatrically and shot and cut as features. *A Rustling of Leaves* was distributed theatrically throughout Canada, the US, Germany and

Britain. *A Place Called Chiapas* played 80 screens in the US alone (in addition to Canada, the UK, Germany, Australia, and elsewhere). And finally, *FIX* had a remarkable theatrical life across Canada when it was toured from coast to coast for the better part of a year. This incredible span of audience and distance is no minor accomplishment, as any practicing independent filmmaker can attest.

Although Nettie Wild has more than once been described as the heir to the mantle of Barbara Kopple, by her own account, she does not consider herself an "activist filmmaker" (although, given the above, "activist distributor," might be more accurate). One might say that rather than making activist films, Wild makes films focused on high-stakes, real life political dramas—not at all the same thing. Overall, Wild's most salient contributions to the genre of documentary filmmaking have come about through her ability to record not events or faces, times or places, but instead to follow movements and to capture the consciousness-building processes that change lives: to capture life moving from what the greatest documentarian of the 20th century Dziga Vertov called "life unawares" to the state of "life aware."

The respect for her energy and her abilities among her filmmaking peers earned Nettie Wild a retrospective at the 2004 Hot Docs Film Festival in Toronto, North America's premiere documentary festival. We are both excited and pleased to extend her that same gesture of recognition to the pages of this monograph series on distinctive Western Canadian filmmakers.

—Brian Ganter, Editor
Education Department, Pacific Cinémathèque
Vancouver, BC, October 2009

Nettie Wild: The Language of the Lens

Interview with Claudia Medina

Nettie Wild: My name is Nettie Barry Canada Wild—thanks to my mum's patriotism—and we are at my house where I have lived for the past twenty-four years.

Claudia Medina: I wanted to start by asking you about your experience as a journalist and your work with radio documentaries and theatre, and get your perspective on how those influenced you, if indeed they influenced you, to become a documentary filmmaker.

Wild: The biggest influence for me has come from theater. It's interesting because when I talk to people who are first getting into film, whether it's drama or documentary, I always recommend that they take an acting course. You might think that that's a really long stretch, between acting in the theatre and directing documentary. But it was my theatre background that gave me a really profound sense of story and of drama.

When you're an actor, you're looking at a script and you're breaking it down into elements that allow you to build drama into a scene. Those elements are exactly the same in fictional drama as they are in documentary. In both, you have characters following some universal story: not the political stories, but the kinds of universal truths that drive us as human beings. It's the story that takes you into the heart of the drama, particularly if it's contradictory. Particularly if you aren't dealing with "heroes" who are saintly, but, who are complicated people, like we all are. As an actor, to get into a scene, you have to understand what drives those complicated people. You also have to understand that without those elements, there's no story, and without story you don't have something that can really pull people into what you are trying to do. So that was huge for me to take into documentary. Out of all of the discussions that I have with my cinematographer, with my editors, with fellow filmmakers, 95% of those discussions aren't talking about financing. They're about drama and how to put the story together. So, the biggest influence for me has been my theatre background.

Medina: How did that relate to your experiences as a journalist? Did you find journalism limiting on that level?

Wild: No, not at all. I come from a family of journalists. My dad was a journalist, my aunt was a journalist, and as a toddler, I literally grew up in the newsroom of the *Vancouver Herald*. That sense of story also came from my father. My dad used to give me a pen every Christmas in my stocking. He would scotch tape one word to it: "WRITE!"

My father was a foreign correspondent, but he had a particular way of going about telling stories, a really intimate, human-interest style. For instance, he chased the story of Gandhi. As a young reporter, that was his big story in India, and it was the personal connection that he had to Gandhi over many years that put my father's stories on the front pages

Net + Dad, nose to nose, 1958. Photo credit: Barry Wild.

of the Fleet Street newspapers. It was that extraordinary personal story that took people into this enormous chapter in Indian independence and British colonial history.

And, you know, my forté in terms of writing my journalistic stories was very much the same thing: finding characters that would take me into places I never could have dreamed of and, with them, facing very, very real, high-stakes dramas.

I think journalism and its deadlines and pressures gave me a good rigour, you know? I have never been afraid of a fact-check. I find a lot of times that people exaggerate facts and figures, depending on what side they are on, to emphasize something. What I learned both from storytelling and theatre, but also from journalism, is to default to the conservative side. I don't mean the conservative side of storytelling or politics, but certainly in terms of the numbers game. For instance, when I was in Chiapas, the government said that there were anywhere between 17,000 to 30,000 government troops deployed to surround the Zapatistas, which is a lot of troops in one state. By the time the left-wing movement got through with those figures—this is no exaggeration—sometimes I would be talking to people who were telling me there were 70,000 troops in Chiapas.

What I knew for sure was that there were a lot of troops down there, right? So I would default to 20,000. Why? Because 20,000 was a lot and it was a number I could back up. I knew that not even the military could come back at me and argue with those figures. It's just lent me a nice sense of rigour which I have taken into my documentary filmmaking.

Medina: Something that's particularly powerful about your films is that kind of broader macro-level, geo-political reality which is very much present in your films, yet still felt through these specific realities.

Wild: I feel strongly that I will only be carried into a story by a character that kind of reaches out and bites me. After that, I can't get that person out of my head. I just think, "What did he do? Then what did she do? And what would I do?" That is what takes me into these big political stories. Believe me, it's not a long checklist of grim and determined issues where

Art Loring and members of the Lax Skiik (Eagle Clan) blockade the logging opera-
tions of the Hobenshields, a family of second generation white settlers.
From: *Blockade*, (Canada Wild Productions). Photo credit: Rob Simpson.

every five years I have got to take on some enormous
upheaval somewhere in the world. It's not that at all. It's
weird, it's like my films choose me. I don't choose them.

Medina: Can you talk a little bit more about that?

Wild: It's not the themes. Honestly, it's not the themes. It's not that
as a political person I'm *not* interested in the fact that there are
a lot of people without rights, or very, very poor in Mexico,
our free-trade partner. It's not that I'm *not* really worried and
not trying to figure out what the hell is going on in the
Downtown Eastside of Vancouver, and every urban city
around the world, in terms of drugs. As a concerned citizen,
of course I'm concerned about those issues. But that's not
what pulls me into making a movie.

Subcommandante Marcos, military leader of the Zapatista guerilla army in Chiapas, Mexico, in a scene from *A Place Called Chiapas*. Photo credit: Frida Hartz.

What pulls me into making a movie, is that I run into people who are living extraordinary lives, and their stories are just incredible. Sometimes they're big newsmakers, like Subcomandante Marcos, and sometimes they are smaller players. Marcos was absolutely responsible for making me pay attention to what was happening in Chiapas. I was pulled down to Mexico by the Zapatistas and Marcos. I wasn't pulled down there because of, you know, what a bind the Mexican government was in, or by the Canadian government for being in a free trade agreement with them. My fascination was the drama of people trying to gain control over their own lives and what they had run up against. Those are the people who I find very intriguing. At that point when I get a really profound sense that the audience is going to be blown away by this story. It's a slam-dunk. I'm in.

Medina: I guess that's what I was referring to with the themes: your fascination with people who are taking control of their own lives in these incredible situations. And the people that you follow *are* extraordinary people. So I am curious as to how you come about finding these people? How does the relationship develop?

Wild: All I know is that until I find them, I'm not interested in making a movie. For instance, with *FIX: The Story of an Addicted City*, the last thing in the world I wanted to do was make another movie about how god-awful it was in the Downtown Eastside of Vancouver. There have been enough of them.

Then I went to a meeting and Ann Livingston, the co-founder of VANDU, the Vancouver Area Network of Drug Users, was in the front of the room, and I had never seen anything like Ann in my life before. Here was a woman, faith-based, madder-than-hell, could out-cuss a logger, standing in front of a room of people, going, "Listen, I don't want to talk about the drug crisis anymore. We know what we have to do. We need a safe injection site, and I'm going to open one. Are you in or out?"

And in that room there were a whole bunch of people whom I had never met before. There were the street nurses, a crown prosecutor whose kid was addicted, and a whole bunch of AIDS activists. I got a buzz in that room that I had only felt when I was in other places in the world when real revolutionary change was about to happen. And now I could feel it, right here, in Vancouver. It was the sense of a birth of a social movement, and I was bitten. That really was when the light bulb went off in terms of a documentary. Not a second before.

Medina: That leads into the next question for me. In *FIX*, the intimacy of getting to know the characters is so deep. You're so completely drawn into these characters, you couldn't have written them. And yet you have to be able to create, or work with, people in a way that allows them to be who they are.

Wild: I don't live in the Downtown Eastside of Vancouver. But the references, the nuances of my city, everything culturally about that scene was familiar (unlike say Chiapas or the Philippines). It meant that as a human being I could go into that situation and establish a very close relationship with not one just person, but three by the end of that film. So we had Ann and Dean, really just peeling like bananas in front of the camera. Why? Because there was an ease, a mutual language that we were sharing. And it wasn't just English. It was cultural. It was the whole works. There was no need for my voice or narration in that movie. Those characters let me in so deeply that the story line, the narrative, could be carried by the characters to the audience. I knew that.

Medina: Is that something you realized as you were shooting, or something you realized in editing?

Wild: We had a pretty strong hunch halfway through the shooting that we were into a story that could possibly unfold without narration. I always try to go without narration. Not because I have a hate-on for narration (I think narration is difficult to do well, but when done well, it is a real storytelling tool). But I always try to see if I can get the kind of intimacy with characters that allows *them* to carry the story without narration.

My other films up until that point had been culturally in another ballpark. I think the access I had in those other situations, although it tended to vary, often wasn't culturally deep enough. So the point of view of all those other films is mine. The narration is my voice, as "the other," going into a situation and doing my very best to cobble together a truth. Not *the* truth, but *a* truth, with characters informing me as much as possible.

What we do formally in terms of the structure of my films which use narration, is that we work really hard at the beginning to get the voice-over to weave key characters into the story. Then we pull back, so that the characters themselves carry the second half of the film and the narration really, really tapers off.

Even though the point-of-view of is mine, I'm not the most important character, and this is something that I think filmmakers, including me, tend to forget: it *is* possible for the point-of-view to be carried by someone who isn't the central figure.

In the case of *FIX*, however, we started to realize that we were so deeply into the intimate lives of these characters we wouldn't need narration. One of the magical things that happened with *FIX* was that as we were looking through the daily rushes, the relationship between Ann and Dean absolutely came up and went, "I'm the movie! I'm the movie!" This was the core of the story, and everything else was secondary. So the dramatic arc of *FIX* is *not* the opening of North America's first safe injection site. The dramatic question of it is: will Dean be able to get off heroin and will he get the girl?

And it's not a trite question: will he get the girl? Because what it's really about is this: can Dean be loved? Anyone who has been a drug user themselves or involved with somebody who is addicted, knows that's a very, very hard thing: to really, really love and be there for somebody who is dealing with a full-on addiction. Addiction and love—those are the two really big profound, dramatic arcs, the real backbone of *FIX*. All of the politics comes for free.

Medina: There is a surprising third character in *FIX*. Was it a decision early on to involve the mayor?

Wild: No. Well, kind of. I couldn't figure the mayor out. At the beginning, I was kind of confused. There was this really straight guy who was the mayor, and he seemed to be talking

Dean Wilson and Ann Livingston in a scene from: *FIX: The Story of an Addicted City.*
Photo credit: Nettie Wild.

this progressive line. But on the other hand, he seemed to be not really acting on it. I had looked at some television news footage of him and it was really boring. He was boring. It was boring. I just thought, "Hmm."

And then one day we followed the Vancouver Area Network of Drug Users in a demonstration into City Hall. So in a funny way they introduced the mayor into the frame. There we were following them and they were hauling this great, huge coffin that was symbolic of all the deaths that had happened from drug overdoses and not having a decent place to go, let alone to inject. So they are hauling this coffin into City Hall and—lo and behold—who is sitting there like a deer caught in the headlights, but Mayor Philip Owen.

Mayor Philip Owen is confronted by demonstrators from the Vancouver Area Network of Drug Users (VANDU). Photo credit: Elaine Briere.

I had this kind of confused idea that we'd better go and talk to him, almost like a courtesy call. We went to his office, and this was a real classic case of, "You shouldn't judge a book by its cover." I went in there and he had never heard of my movies, and I had never voted for him. We were from the total opposite ends of the universe, and he sat me down and asked me if I'd like some tea. I said, "Sure." It was served in this silver tea set, which is real Philip.

I thought in the back of my head, "If we are going to interview this guy we'd better find some interesting way to film it … he should be moving around or something. I said, "Would you be open to just kind of walking around?" And he said, "Sure. Would you like to go to the Downtown Eastside?"

I kind of looked at Kirk Tougas, my cinematographer, and went, "Aces! O.K., yes, of course." I think Philip had five cars at that point because he was this vintage car nut, and he had this really old Cadillac station wagon and we got into it. It was perfect, because it was really big and it didn't make any sound at all, so our sound was pristine.

So we headed to the Downtown Eastside and he started talking about every building, every store. He knew everything. He knew every permit, he knew the lay of the land. He could tell you, "That store over there," he would say, kind of cocking his eye, "says they are selling canned beans." But he had a hunch that there were drugs being run out of it. How did he know? Because he kept a little camera and he would lie in wait in his car. When he saw suspicious activity he would jump out and run into the store and take pictures and kind of confront the guy behind the counter and say, "You say that you are a store but there are only three cans of beans in this store and they are very dusty." Then he would take his photos to the licensing department of City Hall and try and shut them down.

When Philip stepped out of the car that first day we started filming, within thirty seconds he was engaged in a conversation with a guy by the name of Jessie who was fresh out of jail. Philip proceeded to have a very knowing conversation with him about heroin and cocaine, and Kirk and I are kind of looking at each other thinking, "This guy has been down here a lot." He knows the street price of these drugs, he knows that coke is "the bad one" as opposed to heroin—which always gets a laugh in the film from people who think he is being dopey. But, in fact, he's right on the money. And then we realized we had a real character here, and—even better—he loved being on camera. Philip was a showboat but nobody had ever let him be one before. They just thought he was this straight guy with a Saran Wrap smile. So he opened up, and all of a sudden we had this funny, knowledgeable guy who was kind of like your dad.

For a storyteller, that's fantastic, because that means, "Oh man, I'm not only going to be able to make a story for people who think like me, but for my mom and dad, for all the real doubters." Philip was a huge surprise. He took the film into an area that no Hollywood writer could have scripted—a straight guy falling on his sword to open North America's first safe injection site? Couldn't make it up.

Medina: Just the way that the three principle characters interact, or kind of hold each other up within the story is really…

Wild: Yeah it was really fun to see that and quite difficult to stitch together because Philip was careful. Everyone in the Vancouver political scene was so careful. They drove us nuts. It was so Canadian. Philip was saying everything was "fine" and everybody was "working together." And the opposition was basically saying, "Oh, we agree with the mayor" and "He's all wonderful." But we knew darn well that off camera, his own party was stabbing him in the back. But he would never ever admit to that.

That put us as filmmakers in a very difficult position. Because if it's not on film, what do you do? It's very, very difficult to try and tease out what we knew was going on but nobody was actually admitting to on camera. And this is where you get into the rigour thing. This is the big difference between

Nettie Wild, director of *A Place Called Chiapas*, with Major Moises, a commander of the Zapatista guerilla army in Chiapas, Mexico. Photo credit: Art Loring.

documentary and drama. In drama you can sit down and write a new scene. You can fictionalize it and you can show those behind-the-scenes players doing their dirty work, you know? But if you don't have it on film in a documentary, if somebody isn't willing to come forward and actually say it or act on it, you're hooped. Yeah, it's tough.

Medina: What was the dramatic arc in Chiapas, a film where in fact you did use narration?

Wild: In *A Place Called Chiapas*, it's: will Nettie get the interview with Marcos? Now, obviously that's not really a nail biter. I mean that's not really a profound story line. But in that case I wasn't able to get intimate access to anybody. I ended up arguing with Marcos, so that froze me out with him.

Early morning in La Realidad, Zapatista Territory, 1996. Photo: Nettie Wild.

But I was able to get the day-to-day access in the communities. Even though we were arguing, Marcos didn't freeze me out of Zapatista territory, thank heavens. In fact, the most intimate part of *A Place Called Chiapas*, and one of the reasons I think it's—if I can say so—a beautiful film, is because we were able to capture the almost day-to-day character of the land, and the work, and the people, and the struggle down there.

But even the two characters from the North, Manuel and Luciano, who provided us with the real gift (a deep dramatic story), their situation didn't allow us to have really deep access. They were Zapatista sympathizers living outside the official Zapatista zone. Having been ousted from their village by pro-government paramilitaries, we first met them when

A family portrait in Zapatista territory, 1996. Photo: Nettie Wild.

they were living in exile. Two weeks later, we get a little letter that has been sent to us from Luciano saying, "We are going to try to return to our village. Would you like to accompany us?" I remember getting that note. I remember thinking I didn't know whether that letter was two days old or two hours old. We just jumped in a Jeep and went, and when we arrived we were right in the middle of the action. Within hours we were marching back with these people, back to their village to see what awaited them. Extraordinary events unfolded. The state police and the paramilitary groups were waiting for the refugees and us. It was a very tight situation, and we got attacked, the film crew got attacked. Both our crew and the refugees ran. For everybody's security our crew had to leave the mountains.

Zapatista guerrilla and child in Chiapas, Mexico, in a scene from *A Place Called Chiapas*. Photo credit: Elaine Briere.

Ideally, what I wanted to do was to go back and spend time with Manuel and Luciano to find out who the heck these two people were. Find out what kind of lives they led. Move into their day-to-day lives so that we could establish them in the film. We never saw them again. We could never get back there. Sometimes when you are making these films, life does not hand you the perfect scenario where you can spend months getting to know your subjects and then you can organically drift into a deep relationship with tremendous access. When access is not perfect, or deep enough, other decisions have to be made. You have to assess what you *have* on film as opposed to what you had *hoped for.* When we are researching and writing the initial proposal for what we hope to shoot in a documentary, we call the proposal "well-intentioned fiction"—later when you look at your rushes you are dealing with reality. But it isn't the reality of what happened. It's the reality of what you got on film. In the case of *A Place Called Chiapas*, I had only fleeting encounters with Subcommandante Marcos, Manuel and Luciano. The only consistent character throughout the shooting was me. *A Place Called Chiapas*, *A Rustling of Leaves*, and *Blockade* all share this dilemma, and all three evolved into personal cinematic essays with my narration introducing the audience to characters who eventually take me and the audience deeper into the story. They are essays—if you were to analyze it—about really, really extraordinary people.

Medina: I wanted to ask you about *Blockade*, partly because there was a line in your narration at the beginning that struck me. You talked about being in a different culture and about...

Wild: ...being a white girl from the city.

Medina: Yes. So, I'm just curious as to what led you into that story, or how that story found you.

Wild: *Blockade* was absolutely in reaction to the Oka Crisis, which had happened the year before. When Oka happened I was sitting in front of my TV set for twenty, thirty days going, "Oh my goodness, I hope those 2,000 Canadian armed soldiers don't open fire on those Mohawks." That was all I could do. The whole country just sat there paralyzed. It was awful. Night after night after night this terrible standoff was happening.

Afterwards, I thought, "You know what, I'd better figure out where I stand on this, and do something about it." But I knew

I had to have a story, and so I ended up buying my first car and heading out of town. I was particularly pulled north to Gitxsan and Wet'suwet'en territory which was an unusual choice at the time because there was a lot of blockade action happening on the West Coast of Vancouver Island. But back then there wasn't a First Nations voice on those blockades. It was very much the environmentalists standing off against the logging industry.

There were, however, various different, native blockades that had happened in direct response to Oka, but my nose took me to Gitxsan territory. They were in the middle of the most amazing story, which was being played out in the courts, on the land, and in the political arena. They were blockading loggers and battling the biggest court case that Canada had ever seen in terms of sheer square footage (the Gitxan and their neighbours, the We'suwet'en, were claiming 22,000 square miles of territory). The court case was not about money so much. It was not even about whose history was right. Instead, the Gitxsan and the Wet'suwet'en, were demanding that the judge recognize their oral history as legitimate and deserving of a place beside the white colonial history held up by the courts. I was really intrigued by that.

I went up in the territory and started to poke around, and Don Ryan, who was the chief negotiator for the Gitxsan, auditioned me. He took me around in his truck for about a week and half the time he was talking he was speaking Gitxsanimax. I had no idea what he was saying, and when he was speaking English he was talking about, "My mother's name is Gwaans and that woman over there, her great grandmother was a bear…" And I am kind of going:

"What?!" You know, here I am from the city and I was trying not to show how completely clueless I was. After a while, Don and his family said, "O.K., you can film us." I realized I had passed the audition.

And then I had to court the white community up there, which was even harder. They were afraid that I was going to be some liberal Indian lover and that I was going to crucify them in terms of what the message of the film would be.

We ended up following these loggers into the forest and entering their very complicated lives along with those living in the Gitxsan villages. Then the phone rings one morning and I get a phone call from one of our "lead characters." Wing Chief Art Loring is asking me, "I don't know if you are interested in this, but we are going to throw a white family off our land. So do you want to film it?"

That led to one of the most complicated stories I have ever filmed. A story that shone such a light on the nature of who we are in this country. The Frog Clan was evicting a nice, retired couple from Ontario who were building their dream home on land they had bought on the beautiful Skeena River. They had no idea their land was in dispute. According to white law it could be bought and sold. What they didn't know is they were buying land that was a hereditary fishing site. So we film the Frogs as they evict the couple off the land. And then the Frogs are at a meeting. They decide to pay the couple a fair price for the land. Then who shows up at the meeting? The Killer Whale Clan. They say the land belongs to *them*, not the Frogs. And all of a sudden we have a window into a real dispute that touches deep into the Gitxsan heart.

It was interesting because when I went north, I thought, "I'm going to have a nice time in the mountains. I'm going to get back to the land, get back to roots, and it's going to be simple. You know, get back to the simple life. The cities are where all the politics are really happening." What I found is that the politics really rocked out there on the land because whatever happened politically immediately and directly affected the people in those valleys. Those people knew they had to live together, whether they were Indian or non-native, or a mix, so it was hardball, and it was complicated. I really like that. It wasn't academic. Everyone in that frame (of *Blockade)*, whether they were white or native thought that, goddamit, it was their home and native land. The white guys had been there for three generations and the native guys had been there since time immemorial. And the white guys had built the roads and the schools, and the First Nations people had trapped and hunted forever. The stakes were really high.

It was funny, but it renewed a kind of political spirit for me about my homeland; I was more connected there. Politics were just alive, and boy were they embodied in huge stories. The stories up there took me to a place no scriptwriter in Hollywood could ever have dreamt up.

Medina: That also speaks to a commonality that I've seen in a lot of your films. You break through any possibility of sticking to a dogma. You let the people be, as you say, the complicated people they are. It stops being something that I am reading about in a newspaper and becomes something that I can easily and feasibly put myself into.

Wild: I think that's our job as storytellers. But you know, I think the problem with my films is that sometimes they are too complex, I let the canvas get too big. I get too excited about the complications and contradictions, so sometimes I am following too many characters. The story becomes thin.

That was one of the real gifts with *FIX*: we had three characters who let us get in so deep into one story, whereas with *A Rustling of Leaves* or *A Place Called Chiapas*, we were all over, following a huge cast of characters. *Chiapas* works best when the movie finally settles and you are able to follow the refugees going back home.

There is also a danger that the storyline gets stretched because you are covering political points instead of scenes that directly affect and build your characters. Say you want to include a scene because you feel you have to cover the women's struggle, or the U.S. military presence. These are political points, not story points. I hope to God there's very little, if none of that, in our films. But shooting to develop character and *not* necessarily to develop political points often gets me into hot water at public screenings. Not necessarily in the community, but invariably when you are at some big screening the politically correct folks are quick to point out a list as long as your arm of stuff that is not in each film and which, in their opinion, should be.

I remember when we opened *A Place Called Chiapas* at the Berlin Film Festival. This really well-meaning German guy who was a part of the local Zapatista solidarity group stood up in front of a crowd of fifteen hundred people and said, "Where is the women's movement?" and "There should be far more about U.S. involvement in Chiapas." And "Where's this?" And "Where's that?" And I just had to say, "You're right. It's not there. If I could have found a dramatic story during my time there to have carried us into any one of those issues, it would have been in the movie. And that's not to say there isn't a human story that can do that. I just didn't find it at the time and in a way I could film."

A classic case of not finding a compelling way to tell an important element in the story, is in *FIX*. One of the characters who is really underrepresented is Ann Livingston, who is one of the three main characters. It just so happened that every time we interviewed Ann about her back story, her answers became very tired or very, very flat. Other times, she would allude to her past in a very animated way and we didn't have a camera rolling [laughs]. In that particular case, Ann's backstory didn't exist for me in a form that we could work with. We had miles of footage of her explaining her background but it was not told in a way that stood up, so it ended up on the cutting room floor. And because I had made the decision not to use narration, key facts which would have provided a more compelling context for Ann had to be left out.

So that's what I mean: if you don't have the material that takes the political point forward in a successful dramatic way then you can't put it in the movie, because if you do, you'll lose your audience. They will get bored, instead of engaged. And if you lose the audience, you'll lose the show. In screenings, it leads to a lot of political debate, for sure [laughs]. But, it is what it is.

Medina: For me, one of the greatest things about documentary

Dean Wilson, president of the Vancouver Area Network of Drug Users (VANDU) leads a demonstration in the streets of Vancouver's Downtown Eastside. Photo credit: Elaine Briere.

film is that it can incite that kind of debate and engage people in discussion because the answers are not so cut and dried.

Wild: I think that's the big trick: that through story you get people into a place where they are dealing with all sorts of different levels. In that complexity you really learn, and I think story takes you there better than anything. So in *FIX*, you're dealing with a guy who's articulate, who is really smart, and who is also a drug addict. He has a political relationship with a really, really straight mayor, and you get to explore contradictions rather than academically dealing with a list of political points. It leads to really, really interesting discussions.

When I am a filmmaker, when we are in production, I am not an activist. I'm not dissing activists. A lot of times the

Dean Wilson, president of the Vancouver Area Network of Drug Users (VANDU) and Mayor Philip Owen, in the alleys of Vancouver's Downtown Eastside. Photo credit: Lincoln Clarkes.

main characters whom I'm following are activists. But it's not my job—it's *their* job to be the activists. It's *my* job to be the filmmaker. So that means, in fact, I'm completely the opposite of an activist. I'm *not* figuring out what scenes would be good for the movement.

Don't get me wrong, sometimes I hope and pray things go a certain way. But I cannot be a part of what is happening in front

Street nurse Caroline Brunt draws blood from a client in Vancouver's Downtown Eastside. From, *Bevel Up: Drugs, Users & Outreach Nursing,* Directed by Nettie Wild (B.C. Centre for Disease Control and The National Film Board of Canada). Photo credit: Nettie Wild.

of the camera. I have to be able to say at the end of the day that I didn't guide or propose that people do something for the camera. I have to really protect the integrity of the film. Hopefully, we are going to a place that is really extraordinary. My job is to document that real human drama, not help create it.

When the shooting gets really tough, when key characters are facing their biggest contradictions, I can't turn around to the movement and ask, "Is this O.K.?" At times, however, reality means you have to be strategic. Every single day you have to draw a line in the sand. If somebody's life is on the line, of

Street nurse Caroline Brunt brings healthcare to the alleys of Vancouver's Downtown Eastside. From, *Bevel Up: Drugs, Users & Outreach Nursing,* Directed by Nettie Wild (B.C. Centre for Disease Control and The National Film Board of Canada). Photo credit: Nettie Wild.

course you have to stop the camera and say, "O.K. Do you want to be in front of the camera or don't you?" We must have a discussion about how they can be in front of the camera and what that entails. How can they be protected? What are the repercussions? All those things are very, very fine lines, but it is a very different type of discussion than sitting down and going, "This is what the movement wants, and, therefore, I am going to cover this, this, and this."

My last project, *Bevel Up: Drugs Users and Outreach Nursing,* was very different. For the first time I was working as a hired gun.

The street nurses in Vancouver hired me to make an educational, interactive DVD to teach other nurses how to bring better health care to people who use drugs. At the heart of *Bevel Up* is a forty-five-minute, *cinema verite* documentary. In that instance, when we were shooting, I would turn to the nurses and go, "Have we got what you want?" It was very different. People I filmed in my previous films were not in my edit rooms. The nurses, however, screened every cut because of the different kind of relationship I had with them. I was making *their* movie.

However, my other titles are from my point of view. Nettie Wild is entering into a complex, political situation and trying to learn and understand the story as best as I can. I'm making the type of film where one moment I'm with the left-wing New People's Army (in the Philippines) and I know that I'm also going to have to spend time the next day with the right-wing paramilitaries. In that instance, I have to tell the New People's Army, "This is what I'm going to do. Don't freak out when you see me with the paramilitary. I have to understand them as well, I have got to get their heartbeat too." In that instance, you can't have one side, like the New People's Army, in your edit suite. You can't allow one side or the other to call the shots.

I do have private showings for people who have participated in my films when we are starting to get close to a final cut. It's out of respect for our key characters. If they have really opened up their interior life to our camera, then they have the right to see the final version before the public does.

Once the picture is locked, once we are in distribution, then my role can change—I *can* strategize with the movement about how best to get the film seen and then it is fun to work with the activists.

Medina: Can you speak about that in terms of your own strategies around distribution and how you go about it?

Wild: Well it's very simple really. It's about understanding that nobody is going to be able to distribute the films I make with the kind of heart and passion that I can bring to them. A distributor might have twenty-five or fifty titles to distribute. The ones with big Hollywood names will get really excellent distribution. But they will put a film like mine on the back burner. I *can't* put it on the back burner. I come away from every single project having bonded very, very closely with people who have in some cases, put their lives on the line, in order to make the movie.

So my colleague and producer, Betsy Carson, and I distribute it ourselves, as an increasing number of independent producers now do, and we start from a very simple place: "How do we get our films into theaters?" People write political documentaries off as being kind of boring history or news. But I always shot my films because I had a very strong belief that even though they were called political documentaries, the reality is, they are following some of the biggest, high stakes, human dramas of our time. If you shoot them that way and you cut them that way, then you can find an audience. I always worked in a long format, because the stories were big and complicated, but also because they could get into the cinemas. So I would just start from that simple place: "How can I get this darn thing into the theatres?

So I began by literally calling up the handful of cinemas across Canada and then in the United States that were independent art houses. With the first film, *A Rustling of Leaves*, there were very few cinemas that would take it. Gradually that has changed. With our last theatrical movie, we spent more time in chains, in multiplexes, than we did in independent art houses, because we were making them money. Sometimes we screened with Cineplex Odeon, sometimes we were on a Landmark screen, sometimes we were in an independent cinema.

I find it very, very interesting because what's happening with the multiplexes is they've grown too big. What that means is, when a blockbuster opens on a Friday and Saturday, for that first weekend, the majority of the screens in the multiplex will be completely locked down with the new picture. It'll be very difficult for you, as an independent, to get your title into a multiplex on those opening weekends when a blockbuster opens. But other than that first Friday and Saturday night, if you do it right, you can fill your one cinema with more people than in all the other screens in the multiplex combined. That's because you are opening in one cinema in the country at a time and you are focusing the media on just one market. So we're only in Vancouver. We're only in Toronto. We're only in Salmon Arm. Wherever we are, we can often out-box-office everybody else in the multiplex, because the reality is, after the first Friday and Saturday night, the other screens are deader than a doornail on Sunday, Monday, Tuesday, Wednesday, and Thursday. It happens.

Next is what I like to call "new media to support old media." Our little team uses the internet, the new media, to get the word out, and get people to come to the cinema, and in the cinema I get people to work the internet when they get home, to get people to come out. It's like a rinse cycle, and it turns everybody into our alternative publicists.

Then on Friday, Saturday, or Sunday after each seven o'clock show we have a major community event featuring key figures in the film and myself. We end up creating a news event which gets coverage. Because we cannot afford to buy the kind of ads that a mainstream film can, we have to get feature stories on the city side of the paper or the arts pages. And we do that through these events, where we couple someone from the film with somebody from that community who is doing a similar kind of work. You kind of highlight local stars and give the media a local hook.

With *FIX*, this was a really sweet formula. We would find various people—a methadone doctor, or a street nurse, a drug user group, a cop—who were working with drug users or maybe we would find someone railing against them. We called them the "Harm Reduction All-Stars." We would have a rocking debate after the seven o'clock show and that would create a mini *mercado*, a mini market, out in the lobby with people selling stuff, and literature, and all the rest of it. It would create publicity, it would create a buzz.

With *A Place Called Chiapas*, we were distributed by Zeitgeist Films in the U.S. But I travelled with the film throughout the U.S. and worked with the Mexico Solidarity Network. We played over eighty screens. While the box office went to our distributor and funders, during after-screening discussions, we raised over $100,000 US for Zapatista Civilian communities—just by passing the hat.

I like to turn the cinemas back into the village well, and people love it and they go tell the house manager, "This is fantastic, when can we do it again?" The house manager usually starts out thinking, "Oh my God, I'm going to have the director in the house for a week. This is a nightmare." But if I can get the first Friday shows up and running on time, and we don't get in the way of the popcorn line-up, if they have a full house and they're making money at the box office, then they are very happy for the rest of the weekend, and they hold us over.

So you know, it's not rocket science. I still have a lot to learn from people who have distributed theatrically in the last couple years, because there is a whole other way of working the internet. Everything shifts and changes. I am by no means the expert at this point, not in terms of community-based organizing. But that's the fun of it. It's not going to stay the same all the time. If you are self-distributing, the person you want to talk to is the last independent filmmaker who was just out there in the cinemas. They are the new experts.

Medina: In regards to actually screening your films in the communities where you shot them, how has the response been? What kinds of things stand out to you in terms of going back to show the completed piece?

Wild: To take your film back into the community to show it—those are the Rolls Royce screenings. They are the most frightening screenings and they are the most wonderful, the most spectacular. With *FIX* we had a whole run in Vancouver, we had five weeks. That was very, very special.

With *A Rustling of Leaves* I couldn't get back into the

Philippines with the film. But the National Democratic Front (the political leadership for the underground army) was in exile in the Netherlands, and I went there to show it. The leadership came from all over Europe. They wanted to see it because the filming had been controversial within the movement.

It seems with my films there is always controversy. They are not the easiest films to make. I usually end up at odds with some faction or another within the very movement that I've been attracted to, to come down and film. This is a particular kind of hot water I regularly seem to get myself into.

If your characters, the main people you are following, if they end up in a very, very difficult contradictory position, what I really hope for is that I have enough of a relationship with them that they let me keep filming. They may not be looking so heroic anymore. But for me that is gold. It has nothing to do with trying to hang people's dirty laundry out in public. It has to do with the fact that we see what they are up against. It's not a picnic; the stakes are really high.

Inevitably, there is somebody in the political movement—if not a lot of people—who are going, "What are we doing? Why are we letting her film something so sensitive? We are fighting a revolution! We have enough to do without her sticking her camera into our lives." And if I'm really lucky, which I have been in every single film, I've had at least one person in a really key position that has said, "Let her keep filming."

That has meant I have found myself in a really lonely place a lot of times. During the shooting of *A Rustling of Leaves*, the

Communist Party balked at letting me go up into the mountains to film the guerilla New People's Army. The Communist Party is the political organ and the New People's Army is under their control. I had this strong trust and this emotional relationship with the army. But the party was going, "Holy shit, she's in too deep."

The communist leadership said that I had to have a member of the party with me while I was filming, which I went for. Then they said that I had to have a member of the party in the editing room afterwards, which I refused. At which point they not only refused me access to their army in the mountains, but it was hardball. I mean they made it very, very clear that the communist leadership was upset enough to take "measures" if I should attempt to film. I was cut off.

I was trying to get back to the mountains to film the first fighting front of the New People's Army in Mindanao in the southern Philippines. During my research the year before I had been through an extraordinary and difficult experience with them. We had come under heavy attack from the Armed Forces of the Philippines. We had become very close and the guerrilla commanders believed that ultimately, I would not betray them. It was that belief that led them to sneak me up into the mountains, effectively ignoring orders from their leadership in the Communist Party, and that's how we made *A Rustling of Leaves*. I learned a big lesson about how trust and friendship can trump even a military command.

Back in Canada I get the film cut and there are key people in the movement who are really upset that this movie is coming out. In the movie there are some very harsh scenes. Then we

Members of the New People's Army in a scene from the feature documentary, *A Rustling of Leaves: Inside the Philippine Revolution.* Photo credit: Nettie Wild.

get accepted into the Berlin Film Festival. It's a big deal. That's when the Filipino Communist leadership in exile in Europe asked to see the film on my way to Berlin.

I go to Utrecht in the Netherlands, and they pull together all these people throughout Europe who are in exile in different countries. They all come together in this house and I find a

16mm projector and start to show the film. I show the first reel: they love it. It's good cinema, it's showing a really tough situation where poor people are not in control of their own lives. It's explaining and really putting forward why in the world somebody would go underground and join a guerilla army. Second reel: they love it. We start to introduce the paramilitary death squads and what people are really up against. And then there are the third and fourth reels and then we get to the fifth reel.

In the fifth reel, a kid, an indigenous kid who was a part of the guerrilla army, defects, and goes over to the other side. He starts naming key people in the underground to the military. We are all stuck up in the mountains, including myself and my crew, and we keep filming. And then the kid is not treated well by the military. The indigenous boy decides to leave and come home, not really understanding what he's done. He's been finger-pointing. He's actually frozen the entire area. He's put people's lives in jeopardy. And now he decides that he's going to come home.

The revolutionary army captures him and they decide to have a people's court; I film it. There's an assumption by me, and I think by the leadership, that because this kid is seventeen years old this will be a chance to show the movement at its most benevolent, as opposed to the chaotic and heavy hand of the Armed Forces of the Philippines. In the mountains, the people's court happens in this boy's village, and the village comes to the conclusion that he has to be executed. All of that's in the movie, and how events roll out afterwards is in the film.

Two members of the New People's Army in a scene from the feature documentary, *A Rustling of Leaves: Inside the Philippine Revolution.* Photo credit: Nettie Wild.

And now I'm in Utrecht showing this to the leadership and you can hear a pin drop. On top of that, one of the main characters in the film is the guy who started the revolutionary army. Kummander Dante has spent many years in prison and he has been released by the new president, Mrs. Aquino. Dante decides to run as a candidate in the election instead of return to the mountains. We follow the campaign and there's an assassination attempt on Dante's life: all this is woven together in the film.

In the fifth reel, Dante says that armed struggle should be secondary to the democratic struggle, and that's what blew the Communist leadership in Utrecht away. Not the people's court of the kid—that's what I worried about. I thought, "My god they are going to have a heart attack." No, to them it's reality. I mean, what else would the villagers say? But having their ex-commander say that the armed struggle should be secondary? The Communist leadership in that room in Utrecht went nuts. But the founder of the party, Jose M. Sison (Joema) said nothing while everybody else went crazy. I thought, "Oh man…now what's going to happen?"

Joema was known as a very strict, doctrinaire guy, and I thought, "He is going to kill me." He listened to all this. Finally, he stood up. And he says, "If I were to grade this movie…regarding the artistic skills, I would give it 98%." Then he said, "And regarding depicting the people's struggle I would give it 90%." Then he said, "Regarding articulating the program of the National Democratic Front,"…and there is dead silence… "I would give it 76%." Then he said, "Comrades, I think this movie is not made for the Central Committee. I think this movie is made for people outside of the Committee, in the Philippines and outside the Philippines, and maybe we need to be talking to those people." And I just thought, "Hallelujah!"

Medina: I am curious about editing these complex stories. What is the editing process like for you? Has it evolved? Has it changed? How do you approach editing?

Wild: I love it, and it's changed with every single editor. Some people, who are wonderfully talented, and who can edit all their own stuff will often say, "How in the world could you let somebody else in there to edit?" My response is that I can't imagine the editing process without an editor.

I look for a couple things in an editor. First of all, I don't necessarily look for a documentary editor. I look for somebody who can really help me find the dramatic bones of a story. I look for somebody who likes dealing in the abstract. While they should be really rigorous in terms of the structure of the story, they should also have the ability to really dance with picture and sound.

I tend to be a literal kind of a gal. Too much so. So I am drawn towards editors who can really challenge me and push me into experimental cinema in their style of cutting.

I'm not particularly interested in someone who is familiar with the subject. In fact, I've come to understand it is probably pretty good to have an editor who is very new to the subject. What you want is an editor who can see what is in the frame, rather than looking at the footage through the lens of a political agenda. As a director you are so deeply steeped in the process you had to go through to actually shoot the footage, that you often just do not have that distance which is so precious in the editing room. I also want an editor who is looking for the story I am trying to tell, and who is not going, "Oh god, if she would just get out of the room I could just make my own film." I've been straightforward with my editors. I tell them, "This footage may not be perfect, but it's the very best I could get. If you are willing to help me find my film, then I am happy to give you as much creative room as you need as an artist."

I've been blessed with great editors. I like to think that all the people we work with are real film artists. I'm not interested in working with someone who's not working on that kind of level. I think people will come to work with us because they get an opportunity to do that. Our wages may not be what they are earning in the mainstream industry. This goes for the editors in particular—but they get to play! And I get to benefit, I get to learn. They are great relationships.

I look hard for an editor, and I find them in various different places and through different routes. For instance, with Mike Brockington, who edited *Bevel Up*: I really liked his work in an extraordinary piece of drama called *On the Corner*, wonderfully directed by Nathaniel Geary. Mike has everything you want in an editor and he needed it all for *Bevel Up*. It evolved into an interactive DVD which meant that Mike and I were exploring a new kind of storytelling. At the centre of the DVD is a forty-five-minute documentary. Mike cut an in-your-face *cinema verite* journey following a team of street nurses that takes the audience through some of the most intimate scenes I have ever filmed. A sex worker is being tested for syphllis; a drug dealer for HIV/AIDS; a pregnant mother, high on crack, is hiding under a trailer with *her* mother who is near death's door with suspected endocarditis and is withdrawing from heroin. The documentary rocks through its *verite* stories without stopping for interviews. That was saved for the menus—three hours and forty-five minutes of interviews with twenty-six experts in you name it— everything from brain chemistry and nursing ethics, to the relationship between the price of street drugs and the sex trade. Mike was just as at home cutting animated sequences of colliding cocaine neurons as he was sculpting darkly dramatic scenes in Vancouver's Downtown Eastside. It was a *tour de force* of editing, all four and a half hours of it.

When I was looking for an editor for *FIX: The Story of An Addicted City*, I saw *Hard Core Logo*. I thought it was a very dynamic cut, and approached Reg (Reginald Harkema). He had only cut one documentary before mine. He also came with quite a reputation in terms of being a strong, opinionated person in the editing room. But Reg was fantastic. He was like a puppy. He came eager to learn how to cut a documentary, because cutting a documentary, according to Reg and other editors I speak to, is a bigger challenge than cutting dramas. It's much harder to make the story arcs work.

After Reg had been working for five months slugging through all our footage, we finally got a rough assembly. He turned to me and said, "If I was cutting a drama, this is where I usually am on day one of shooting—cutting the selected shots into a rough assembly. And we've been cutting *FIX* for five months!" So it gives you a real idea of where the story comes from in documentaries. Of course, you are getting all the colours of the palette when you are shooting on location, but the edit room is really where you are massaging the story into shape.

Manfred Becker, who cut *A Place Called Chiapas*, had just come off another documentary, *Gerrie and Louise* (directed by Sturla Gunnarsson and shot by Kirk Tougas, who also shot *Chiapas*). I had really liked the dramatic structure of that piece, and Manfred proved to be a really exceptional editor in terms of dealing with the experimental frame. He was also phenomenal in terms of sound editing and was really able to create a great soundscape. He laid a tremendous bedrock for Velcrow Ripper, who came in and did the sound design and built on top of Manfred's work. Velcrow is the first person to credit Manfred with really coming up with a very different sounding, unique soundtrack. The sound mix with Danielle Pellerin and Velcrow for *A Place Called Chiapas* was one of the most heady, creative experiences I've ever had as an artist; it was fantastic.

I have a funny story about how different editors can be. The guy who edited *A Rustling of Leaves* was Peter Wintonick. I had never met Peter, and, at that time, Peter Katadotis was the head of the National Film Board. Katadotis had suggested that Wintonick would be a good editor and that he, Katadotis, would fly Wintonick out to Vancouver if I would considering hiring him. Then Peter Wintonick arrived in my life. He is a very extraordinary individual and brings his own particular charm and chaos with him.

We sat down in the editing room and he asked me how I saw the first sequence of the film and I didn't have a clue. I was really a baby filmmaker and he was very patient. So we kind of worked it out with cards on the wall. Then I sat down next to Peter and waited for him to start editing the first scene we had discussed. And nothing happened. Peter kind of talked, and got a little quiet, and…nothing happened. I went out of the room for something and then I heard the Steenbeck starting up and I went, "Oh." Then I went back in, sat down and…he stopped. I went out and the Steenbeck started up again and I went, "Oh, O.K., this is what you do with an editor. You leave them alone!"

At the end of the first day I went into the edit room and I looked at what he cut together, and it was so much more than what we had discussed. It was the sugar cane cutting sequence which eventually opened the film. It was the work of an extraordinary artist who had really gone to town with the footage and it was a beautiful sequence. I was just stunned. And that's how I dealt with Peter. I would give him notes and then leave the editing room, and he would just create this magic.

Next film I was dealing with Jeff Warren, a really established editor who came in to cut *Blockade*. He had cut Sturla Gunnarsson's *Final Offer*, which I thought was really beautifully edited. So Jeff came in and I set him up, and left the room, and he worked away. I came back and gave him notes and left the room again. Finally, Jeff looked at me and said, "When are you going to come and sit beside the editing bench?" I said, "What are you talking about?" And he said, "Well, I'd like you right here." And he pats the chair next to him. So for *Blockade* I spent the entire time there. I actually used to sleep with my head on the Steenbeck—take little naps there. That's how he liked to work. He liked to have the ability to check in with me from moment to moment, and he liked the company.

So for me the relationship with the editor is new every time. This is an extraordinary partnership. I find it harder to find that partnership in sound designers. I wish Velcrow wasn't as successful in his own films and would keep to sound designing for the simple, selfish reason that I think he is a really extraordinary designer to work with and I loved working with him.

Medina: You have a passion for sound editing and strong opinions about the care and the art needed to create a good soundscape, can we talk about that?

Wild: I think all of us are being beaten up by how television has affected documentary, but sound in particular is really taking it in the chops. Sound designers—or sound cutters as they call them—all seem to be working in television these days. And television, in general, brings a certain sensibility which gives short shrift to sound. In their defense, the budgets sound editors get to work with are getting smaller and smaller and, therefore, the time and the care is just not going into the craft. It's very literal, and people are really making sound*tracks* and not sound*scapes*. They are pasting music over sequences, music that tells you how to think. They are not understanding that if you move into the abstract with sound, it's a wonderful world and it can really expand your frame: it's not just see a dog and then hear a dog. I find that this whole idea of going into a mix with the equivalent of 110 or 120 tracks of generic sound effects that a SFX editor has laid down in case you need them—I find it difficult. Instead, I look for a sound editor who is prepared to really sculpt a sound design ahead of time, understanding that every sound is like music. I look for someone who has the courage and the ear to move into the abstract, instead of always staying in the concrete. Then the mix is a joy, not a trial to get through.

But for the most part, mixes are torturous. They are underfunded, there's never enough time, people are settling for less. You come in as a director and you want to work a moment, and you don't have the budget or the political will of the sound studio to really do it. Yeah, I find it very, very difficult. The trick comes in breaking through those dynamics in the mix and trying to get people excited about being artful in that moment. I'd have to say for the most part I think we've been pretty successful, but man, it's a struggle.

Medina: I can certainly see why directors get excited about working with dynamic mixers who really get it.

Wild: Oh, yeah. You know, there aren't that many fantastic mixers, and I think sometimes they just get it mixed out of them. I just think that's there's so much work going through on such limited budgets that everybody is settling for less. "Faster is better." And it shows.

Medina: Somewhat related to that, I'm curious also to know how you see the transition in filmmaking from analog to digital. You worked in film, working on the Steenbeck…

Wild: Well, I love the new systems. I mean I don't ever want to go back to the Steenbeck. Not that I have the talent to be a good editor on a Steenbeck or on an Avid. But today's editing systems are spectacular in their flexibility. In terms of the quality of image, working in film for me is like working in oil paints. It's gorgeous and expensive. Shooting on digital is like working in watercolour. It can be beautiful too. But it's different. So you have to choose what medium you want (or can afford to shoot in): oils or watercolour.

The last film we shot on film was *A Place Called Chiapas*. It just really felt like we—Kirk and I—were painting. There was a lot of digital starting to happen at that time and we made the decision to stick with film. It was a no-brainer. The light and the culture in Chiapas was so rich. Some of the images Kirk got on film were just like paintings. They were so phenomenal. And then we shot *FIX* in digital video and part of that was a financial decision. I think in terms of the look, it was O.K., but there are huge frustrations. And, face it, some of those frustrations came from the low price bracket we were working in, too.

Our transfer to 35mm in *FIX* was heart-attack city. Take a simple thing like a pan, which is an important part of the language of documentary film. In *FIX*, you are panning around the council chamber at City Hall, and you really want the audience to understand that this council member is for the mayor and this person is not. Maybe this one is stabbing the mayor in the back. So you're panning deliberately at a certain pace to really take people through characters, and you're doing it hand-held because you've walked in on the tail of a demonstration that's broken into the council chambers. You put that all together and it's hell for the transfer to 35mm— absolute hell! The digital information that is having to be transferred over to film is changing all the time, because the camera is not locked down and a simple pan is very difficult. So it was funny, it was at the point when we had to transfer the digital image back to 35mm film for theatrical distribution, that we ran into the two mediums clashing with each other. Those pans in *FIX* still really look like hell. The people who did the transfer said it was the hardest one they'd ever done.

I would like to be able, as a filmmaker, to stay in film for some projects. I think that digital has led to shooting like you are turning on a vacuum cleaner. You never turn the camera off and so you shoot yourself in the foot. When we shot *A Rustling of Leaves* we had 64,000 ft. of film (twenty-seven hours) and we were told that was outrageous—it was crazy to shoot that much. I shot three hundred hours of video with *FIX*! So that meant that a great part of the expense of the edit in *FIX* was wading through the material. I think we have to relearn how to shoot, to be more disciplined. But then there's the other side of it, because sound and image are together on video.

You are often really rolling for sound, so that's the equivalent of telling your sound recordist to keep rolling for important voice over dialogue while you turn off your film camera.

Another thing that's a real booby trap with digital is that directors fool ourselves into thinking we can all do it ourselves, and we can't. At least 99.9% of us can't. For example, I have an A crew and a B crew. The A crew is Kirk Tougas on camera with an assistant, so that Kirk can focus on camera and not on carrying the tripod or getting the tapes lined up. If we're shooting digital there's a proper sound person who's making sure that if you're on a lavalier mic—great. If you're on a radio mic—great. Then you always have to have a boom going, really looking out and shopping around for those sounds that will create the "music" for your soundscape. Then there's me as the director, and a production assistant who is running around getting release forms and making sure traffic doesn't run over you and all that kind of stuff. The B crew is me.

Kirk has gradually taught me how to shoot. Now I share a cinematography credit in *FIX*, but man we paid! We gained in that I would be there at three in the morning when Dean was ranting and raving. We would get that moment. But inevitably something would give, and a lot of times it would be the sound, and we would pay in post-production. And that's also how you end up with miles and miles of not particularly inspired shooting. So it's a mixed bag; it's a liberation to shoot on your own but you can also shoot yourself in the foot.

Medina: Tell me about the relationship you've developed with your cinematographer Kirk Tougas, because he's been your main partner in so many ways. How has that developed and changed through time and what that has meant as a filmmaker to have that kind of relationship?

Wild: At one point, I went to New York because I was looking for a crew to shoot what turned out to be my first big film, *A Rustling of Leaves*. I think I was just naïve and I thought I needed a more seasoned crew than I could find in Vancouver. I got a hold of Barbara Kopple. She's used every camera person in the universe in the course of any one of her films. I went to see various people who had shot for her and I remember talking to one of her cinematographers and he said, "I just want to get this right. You don't know me, I don't know you. And you want me to go to the Philippines and put my life on the line for little or no money?" And I kind of said, "Yeah." And he said, "I'm not going to do that." He said, "Don't be a dope, go home and work with your friends, and learn with them, that's what I did." I ended up going home and Kirk agreed to come to the Philippines. He recruited Gary Marcuse as sound recordist and he turned out to be a pacifist! Both Kirk and Gary balked at joining me on military maneuvers with the New People's Army in the mountains, but they still wound up sharing a meal of goat stew with armed partisans and pushing aside M-16's to find a place to sleep on the floor. We were just babies, and we learned together. *A Rustling of Leaves* was a very, very big film, it was way bigger than we were. We had no idea what we were stepping into…

Medina: That was probably a good thing…

Wild: [laughs] I think so…Kirk has shot every single documentary

Crew of *A Rustling of Leaves* at the Berlin Film Festival. From left to right: Robin Bain (Graphics), Rob Porter (Music Producer), Joan Churchill (Graphics), Peter Wintonick (Editor, Associate Producer), Christopher Pinney (Executive Producer), Nettie Wild (Director), Kirk Tougas (Cinematographer). Photo credit: Kirk Tougas.

I've done and he's taught me how to shoot. I remember all sorts of stuff in the beginning. We were frustrated with each other. I think we fought more back then. Now the conversation is kind of like a married couple in that he can start the sentence and doesn't have to end it because I know where he's going. It's very handy when you are in tough situations; when your brain is somewhere between the two of you. That's wonderful and that's why we keep working together; it is a shared language.

In the past, Kirk has made his own experimental films so he has a very fresh, wacky, wonderful eye. So with Kirk, I get

Crew of *A Place Called Chiapas*: clockwise, left to right: Nettie Wild (director), Kirk Tougas (cinematographer), Fransicso Trujillo (translator), Betsy Carson (producer), Robin Lupita Bain (camera assistant extraordinaire), Manfred Becker (editor). Photo Credit: Gary Marcuse.

coverage, but we'll get lots of weird shit too. That's what gives the editor the footage to play with, to provide pacing… depending on the editor. Sometimes you can have a mismatch and that's difficult to deal with. There was one editor who just really didn't get Kirk's style and thought it was irresponsible. And then you give Kirk's work to someone like Manfred Becker (who edited *A Place Called Chiapas*) and Manfred is in heaven, because Manfred has a way of taking Kirk's wilder footage and really dancing with it, and that's terrific. That's when magic happens.

The thing that's really amazing about Kirk is he rarely says,

"Do you want the frame this way, or do you want the sticks over here?" I mean on occasion he will, but what he usually turns around and says to me is, "What character are we following?" And we will figure out how to shoot for the editor not just in terms of coverage, but in terms of story structure.

When I shoot interviews with Kirk, I have my head right next to his lens so that the person I'm filming isn't looking a foot-and-a-half off axis.

And while we're shooting, we'll have this extraordinary exchange. For instance, every now and then I'll get in a situation where I'm questioning somebody—particularly when we're interviewing someone who is perhaps from the "other side"—and it's tense. In the middle of all that, Kirk will often be firing off a little question under his breath that he thinks that I've missed. Or he can sense I'm stumbling, like he can hear my brain worrying away and he'll fire it in. And sometimes I go, "Oh screw you, I've already thought of that or I was just going to go there." But most of the time I'm going, "Thank God." So that's extraordinary.

Kirk has drawn the line with me, on certain occasions, which has infuriated me. I felt terribly betrayed when he told me he would not go up into the mountains with the guerrilla army in the Philippines because he thought he was going to die [laughs]. He was very clear about that. Deep in my heart I really didn't believe he would go back to Canada and leave me in the mountains, but he did. But before he did, he gave a whole series of sweaty workshops (it was a billion degrees, outside and in) to myself and Jojo Sescon on how to work the Aaton camera. Jojo was this wonderful stills photographer from the Philippines who wanted to be a DOP [Director of Photography] and became one in that moment. Kirk taught the two of us how to shoot and then he got on a plane and left.

However, Kirk did shoot valiantly when we were not in the mountains, but instead were filming the so-called legal side of the story in the Philippines. One time we were interviewing this right wing radio DJ, Jun Pala, who was aligned with the death squads. At one point Pala started to threaten to kill us, and Kirk, under his breath was going, "It's a cut, let's get the fuck out of here!" And I was going, "But he's saying it on camera!" And this was all without Kirk or I moving our lips while we were whispering back and forth.

When I think of our relationship, it's hilarious.

I remember another time during the Philippines shoot, we were chasing after the body of this labour union organizer whom Pala had threatened on the radio. The organizer had been killed, and we figured this particular paramilitary group, which we suspected was working with the Philippine Military, was responsible. We also had heard that the military might have the organizer's body. We figured the paramilitary and the Armed Forces of the Philippines were working in cahoots with each other, so we went up to this military fort—it's in the movie—and we had written "PRESS" on the window which was supposed to impress everybody.

As we pulled up to the fort where the military was, we saw some soldiers treating a man not very nicely at all. In fact, they were torturing him, and as we pulled up the guy ran away from the soldiers and ran straight towards us, and the military opened fire. So Kirk jumps out of the Jeep and the sound man is trying to get his stuff together. I am out of the Jeep next to Kirk. There's like [bullet sounds] everywhere with dust jumping up where the bullets are hitting, and Kirk hits the dirt. I'm going, "Kirk, roll!!" And he turns around and he goes, "Fuck off!!!" [laughs]. He was spreading himself as thin and low as he could on the ground which we thereafter called the "Kirk Tougas School of Cellophane Cinematography." The sound man was crouched down in the Jeep but he had his boom pole poking up like a periscope [laughs]. It was so funny. So yes, we have shared extraordinary times together.

In *A Place Called Chiapas*, I actually got Kirk into the mountains. Kirk would rather be in the *Café de Paris* in Paris than up in some mountain somewhere. Anyways there he was, and the roads up there are actually rivers, and hopefully when you're in them, they are just creeks. While we were filming a monsoon hit and we had to come back. We were going through what used to be a creek and it's now a river and it's up to our chests and we were carrying our camera gear on top of our heads. So there's poor Kirk with his Aaton balanced on top of his head.

I remember with *FIX* we ended up in Europe at a safe injection site and Kirk turned to me at one point and said, "You know, other directors take me to beautiful museums or we go to vineyards or document musicians who play beautiful music. With you I end up getting shot at or in safe injection sites. Any chance you are going to lighten up?" [laughs] It's been a very good relationship, and Kirk together with all my editors have taught me filmmaking. That's where I've learned how to put a story together: we've learned together.

Medina: And when you look back on those films you have made together, are there any lessons learned about your role as a filmmaker?

Wild: When I was starting to make films, the whole politically correct, cultural appropriation argument was around. For me, one good thing however did come out of it, besides a lot of pinched filmmaking, and that was this: I ask myself every day I am shooting, "What the heck am I doing here?" I started to understand after a few films what my role was, and that it was O.K. to be filming far from home. There is indeed a role for an outsider's curiosity to come into a community as long as you question your motive every step along the way. You don't come with an arrogance, but instead with a real hunger for knowledge. If you do that, there is a place for you.

And I've found there is an even bigger role (because of the part that North America plays in terms of the power politic), to bring the story back home and make sure people in our backyard hear the story. This is a big part of the social contract between myself as a filmmaker and the people I film. That's what has led me, after every film, to spend a year on the road distributing it, and distributing it well so that a lot of people see it.

Many, many people participate in my films for one very profound reason. Some of them even put their lives on the line for one very simple and harsh reason: other people, outside their village or town, don't know they exist, let alone that they are in trouble, or their lives are on the line. They know they might die without anyone knowing they ever lived. Somebody goes to a labour meeting in the Philippines and doesn't come home. Who's to know? And that's where I think our job as filmmakers comes in. If someone puts their life on the line in order for you to tell their story, well then—you just can't come home and complain about Canadian distribution not being any good. Nuh-uh, it's not on. You've got to deliver.

And this leads to another important point, I think, which is figuring out who the ideal audience is. You know how everyone always asks that uncomfortable question: "Who are you making your movie for? Who is your ideal audience?" And we always say, "Everybody!" because we want everybody to look at our films. But I do know exactly who I make my movies for. I make my movies for the person who *I* was *before* I knew anything about that particular area or that particular subject.

Take *FIX* for Example. When I first started shooting, I thought VANDU (Vancouver Area Network of Drug Users) was an oxymoron. I thought, "How could you organize drug-users, because they are so out of it? How could you do that?"

So I made *FIX* for that well-meaning, but dumb, girl who didn't know that—of course, people who use drugs can be organized and have a voice. Before making *FIX*, I had totally bought into what our community put out there, which is that you are either on drugs or you're off, and only when you're off can you get better. I just didn't get it. I didn't understand that you could pursue better health and still continue to take drugs. Understanding that is the whole philosophy of *harm reduction*. But I'm not going to make a movie about harm reduction. That's like making a movie about the twelve-point program of the Zapatistas—you'll put people to sleep.

Instead, with *FIX*, I thought, what if I make a film about Dean Wilson—who is this rip-snorting, smart, and really addicted drug user—and Ann Livingston—who doesn't touch a drop of anything? If they are both organizing to open North America's safe injection site (and maybe they are having a relationship but you're not quite sure) then all of a sudden we're talking about a really fascinating human story. I know I'm reeled in, so I know I can reel in people who have never been to a drug and alcohol meeting. I am making that movie for that well-meaning, naïve girl. I know that girl and I know she has a heart. So if I can tell the story to a lot of people who are in that same position as I was, then that's a very specific audience.

I want to get a roomful of people like that to a place where they look at a really complicated situation—whether it's in the Downtown Eastside of Vancouver, or in Chiapas, Mexico, or northern B.C., or the Philippines, or wherever—where I can have them sit there and go, "Shit, what would I do if I was there?" That's all I want to do. I just want to get my audience right there because then the rest is up to them. I just have to tell my story really well. That's my job.

Interview transcription by Natalie Clager.

1. See Aufderheide, 2007.

2. For background on the history of the term "new political documentary" see Benson and Snee, 2008.

3. A detailed overview of the complexities of the production, filming, and financing of *A Rustling of Leaves* can be found in Chapter 3 ("Hold on to the Horses") of Michael Posner's *Canadian Dreams: The Making and Marketing of Independent Films* (1993).

4. These terms are Gerard Genette's and he discusses them in his collection of essays, *Narrative Discourse* (1983).

Wild at Heart

BY MARK HARRIS

I.

As Nettie Wild knows full well, the problem of authenticity has haunted the art of nonfiction filmmaking from the very beginning. To figure out how we, the [collective] viewer, can know this about her, the [solitary] director, it will first be necessary to provide a fair degree of historical background to confirm this contention, since the documentary feature's pedigree is even more complicated than that of its narrative counterpart.

Years before Georges Méliès faked the coronation of Edward VII in 1902 and the Lumière brothers accidentally invented slapstick comedy in *L'arroseur arrosé* (1895), even the least contrived slices of everyday life were laced with fictional elements. For instance, in the North Korea of Kim Il Sung, did any workforce ever leave its factory in a fashion as orderly as that of the lens grinders in *Sortie des Usines* (1895)? Obviously, the Lumières did far more than just establish the width of commercial film stock (35mm) and adopt the Renaissance perspective of Leon Battista Alberti (a tradition pursued by every subsequent cinéaste, with the partial exception of Yasujiro Ozu). In Jean-Luc Godard's *La Chinoise* (1967), it is brilliantly argued that, not only were the brothers painters rather than filmmakers (their subject

matter being the same as that of the nineteenth century Impression-
ists), but that history has turned *them*—not their great contemporary
Georges Méliès—into the true fathers of fictional filmmaking , not
least because the events of the latter's most famous film (*Le voyage dans
la lune* [1902]) were fated to be broadcast live over U.S. TV (albeit in
a much less sensational manner).

Documentary, in other words, is not synonymous with truth.
Indeed, it is open to so many different kinds of manipulation, it
frequently beats fiction at its own *trompe l'oeil* game.

Of course, initially, the filmmaker's capacity to "lie" was very
limited. When you only have 30 seconds worth of film stock to play
with, and no editing capacity to speak of, photographing a train
arriving at La Ciotat station was about as far as a documentarist could
be expected to go. With montage, however, at the turn of the century,
came greater opportunity. Thus, the audiences of a hundred years
ago were able to see footage of the 1905 San Francisco Earthquake
that was not all that different from the televised coverage of the 9/11
attacks (not surprising really, since the newsreel is the direct ancestor
of the nightly newscast).

In the early 1920s, avant-garde artists such as Man Ray and
Fernand Léger were able to combine experimental cinema with
standard documentary practice in such innovative works as *Ballet
Mécanique* (1924) and *Emak-Bakia* (1927). This development was more
or less contemporaneous with the ascendency of the so-called "city
film," condensed dawn-till-dusk studies of Europe's Jazz Age capitals
(of which Dziga Vertov's 1928 masterpiece *Man with a Movie Camera* is
the prime example even though, ironically, it is a feature that deals
with more than one metropolis).

Ethnographic cinema came of age in 1921 with the success of
Robert Flaherty's *Nanook of the North*, while John Grierson would
subsequently try to impose a bourgeois face on propagandistic short

subjects, first with the British Empire Marketing Board and General Post Office, and then with the National Film Board of Canada (NFB).

Sadly, as an art form, documentary probably reached its apogee in Leni Riefenstahl's *Triumph of the Will* (1935), even if, as a means of honest communication, it also reached its nadir. That this big budget, high-tech record of the Nuremberg Congress and rallies is thoroughly imbued with Nazi ideology cannot be denied, even if, as some apologists claim, the aesthetics owe more to Albrecht Speer (who had been ordered by Hitler to construct buildings that would decline into "magnificent ruins" 1,000 years hence) than they do to Joseph Goebbels (who may or not have been Riefenstahl's arch enemy in the upper echelons of the Third Reich).[1] Susan Sontag, to mention just one important naysayer, was unwilling to cut world cinema's most notorious neo-pagan even this much slack, as she proved in her famous essay, "Fascinating Fascism").[2]

Needless to say, the outbreak of the Second World War greatly expanded the political need for nonfiction cinema—indeed, without it, the NFB might never have come into being—and all belligerent powers sent cinematographers to the front in unprecedented numbers. This trend was particularly true of the Soviet Union, where hundreds, perhaps thousands, were killed in action between 1941 and 1945. The movies of the postwar period would be permanently changed by the fact that so many fictional filmmakers had been exposed to far more "reality" than any sane human being should have been expected to endure (seeing colleagues die under fire is not, incidentally, an experience with which Nettie Wild is entirely unfamiliar, a subject to which we shall return at the proper time).

In the late 1950s and early 1960s, Jean Rouch began to free ethnographic documentary from its colonialist mindset by asking his subjects what they thought of their onscreen representations, and re-cutting his films accordingly. Ironically, this moral house-cleaning co-existed with what was probably the sleaziest documentary tradition of all time, the Italian *Mondo Cane* school that sought to titillate Westerners with the sight of Third Worlders behaving as wickedly and perversely as possible.

Lightweight 16mm cameras and sound recording devices made possible the documentary breakthroughs of the late 1950s and early 1960s (known variously as *cinéma vérité*, *cinéma direct* and Free Cinema, depending on the locality, but all basically following the same hand-held, in-the-street-and-in-your-face aesthetic). This multi-faceted school opposed voice-over narration (the cornerstone of Griersonian documentary) and argued that subjects should be allowed to speak for themselves. Voices of the dispossessed were treated with esteem, especially in the UK (where the radio documentaries of the 1940s, especially those scripted by Dylan Thomas, were leading Britons to expect a brighter future for returning Second World War vets, a future that largely failed to materialize) and Quebec (where *cinéma direct* was closely allied with first the Quiet Revolution of Jean Lesage, and then the sovereigntist movement of René Lévesque).

Curiously, despite the central presence of Leni Riefenstahl and the understandable reluctance of government-subsidized cineastes to directly challenge the status quo—to a greater or lesser extent, their livelihoods obviously have always depended upon it—nonfiction cinema has always appealed overwhelmingly to left-wingers. It was perhaps not coincidental that Lenin considered filmmaking to be the most important of the arts. The unprecedented box office successes of Michael Moore, whom his detractors have accused of inventing the "crockumentary," would not have been possible if not for the groundwork laid by Barbara Kopple, Frederick Wiseman, Chris Marker, Joris Ivens and a host of other iconoclasts whose works have little in common with the more conformist commercial film industry. That these "troublemakers" sometimes win Oscars can be explained by the fact that their work is nominated by fellow documentarists; if, say, Charlton Heston had been in charge, the Academy's laureates would have shared a very different aesthetic.

So much for the world as a whole. What about Canada as a unique case study?

That documentary should have played such a major role in the development of our national identity can, with equal ease, be seen as either unexpected or unsurprising. It's unsurprising inasmuch as our country's vast land mass and relatively small population base make the theoretical notion of a unifying factor rather different from that of our powerful neighbour to the south; and it's unexpected to the degree that the country's political status is anything but clear-cut, never mind bumptiously jingoistic. As a dominion, Canada fell somewhere between an independent nation and a self-governing colony of the United Kingdom. With the notable exception of Quebec, the population was originally so homogenous that the distinction between "homeland" and "mother country" was nebulous to the point of non-existence (we'll be returning to the subject of Canada's "second nation" shortly).

Thus, when emigration from Eastern Europe was encouraged at the dawn of the twentieth century, the Canadian Pacific Railway hired foreign documentarists to make farming the virgin soil of this semi-colony's newly incorporated prairie provinces seem all but irresistible to poor, potential Caucasian immigrants (the Dominion still being officially a "white man's" country). As was so often the case in Canadian history, this move was partially predicated on the need to keep national territory out of American hands, although this was not patriotism in the usual sense of the word. More particularly, it was part of a program to keep Canada "British" or, at the very least, as British as circumstances would allow. It should not be forgotten that the distance between Victoria and Halifax is approximately twice that of the expanse between Halifax and London. With modern communications still in their infancy, keeping things together was no mean feat.

Initially, this job was left primarily to the provincial film boards, the first of which was founded in Toronto in 1917, at which time the Ontario Government Motion Picture Bureau continued the CPR's tradition of farming film work out.[3] Others followed, including one—the Canadian Motion Picture Bureau—that was at least theoretically federal (Newfoundland, being pre-Confederation in those days, played no part in this history). Such flimsy bonds of national unity were similar to the reassurance offered by chartered banks and a handful of Canadian owned trans-national corporations (the CPR, the Hudson's Bay Company, etc.). Limited in scope though they unquestionably were, without these distinctions, Canada would have been pretty much indistinguishable from an exceptionally large, unusually variegated island in the Scottish Hebrides.

When the National Film Board was founded in 1939, most of the original staff had come from the British Isles (with Caledonians predominating, as seemed natural in those days). When asked about forming a francophone wing, John Grierson did not initially see the need for hiring any Québécois staff at all (although he probably *didn't* rule out the possibility of employing General de Gaulle's Free Frenchmen, especially the ones who had previously been employed by Gaumont and Pathé). This cultural enrichment would have to wait for a number of years, while the separation of the ONF from the NFB would be delayed by close to two decades. Much animosity emerged from Grierson's short-sighted—and internally colonialist—perspective, a breach that not even the 1956 transfer of the Film Board's main offices to Montreal could heal.

As for commercial documentaries, they were painfully rare, and those that did exist were most mostly produced by "Budge" Crawley's modestly endowed company, a production house that occasionally dabbled in fiction and animation as well, until it folded in 1982. Trust-busting is not a Canadian invention, and this country has never been notably allergic to media monopolies; in this last respect, our home and native land was shamefully ahead of the rest of the world.

The establishment, first, of CBC TV and then, some nine years later, of CTV, obviously opened new opportunities for Canadian documentarists. The same could be said for the subsequent explosion of cable stations, although far less than the sheer economic scale of this expansion would suggest (in the five hundred channel universe, *Seinfeld* re-runs are seemingly playing on 499 of them more often than not).

This said, for most Canadians, the NFB and documentary filmmaking remain pretty much synonymous, which is ironic under the circumstances. In the 1950s, 16mm Film Board shorts played in every classroom in the country and their ubiquity on U.S. screens (back in the days when "short subjects" were part of every complete motion picture package) caused American documentarists to complain about unfair competition (to the best of my knowledge, the only time this has ever happened in America, if radically different— and inherently unjust—foreign and domestic censorship restrictions are left out of the equation). Given a relatively free hand, these highly productive NFB cineastes racked up outputs that were so protean, they are almost impossible to classify. For example, an NFB staffer credited with directing a "mere" fourteen films might have been the sound editor on sixty-five more, the principal cinematographer of fifty-seven others, the producer of a further fifty-one, the author of thirty-eight screenplays with which he or she had no further connection, and the inventor of seven new pieces of cinematic technology, all of these accomplishments being achieved during the hours when said employee was not working in his or her official capacity as publicist or researcher. The strict craft lines of the Hollywood production system were never followed, and it seems almost certain that, in its heyday, the NFB gave Canadians more "bang for their buck" than any other organization in the nation's history, either private or public.

Of course, there *were* limitations. NFB directors were expected to put a *positive* spin on the Canadian experience, and those who did not frequently ran into trouble. This situation became particularly acute when big business was involved. Thus, from the mid-1960s onwards, the Board has done a fairly good job of, say, documenting the systematic discrimination conducted against First Nations people. Its willingness to name names when it comes to tackling irresponsible companies, conversely, is feeble to say the least. The tragic fate of Denys Arcand's *On est au cotton* shows what happens when the villain ceases to be amorphously societal and becomes concretely corporate. One *could* describe it as a blacklisting, I suppose, but that would oversimplify what actually happened; as always in such circumstances, in order to avoid the appearance of overt repression, the federal government played a complicated game of smoke and mirrors.

In other words, those who would cross swords with well-connected giants generally need to look for different "armourers."

II.

So how *does* Nettie Wild fit into this extraordinarily intricate cultural matrix? Well, as one might expect from someone who was both born in New York and given the middle name of "Canada," the answer is "petty darn well, thank you"… even if the fit is somewhat tangential. In her four, full-length documentaries (*A Rustling of Leaves: Inside the Philippine Revolution*; *Blockade*; *A Place Called Chiapas*; and *FIX: Story of an Addicted City*), this politically engaged filmmaker has taken full advantage of the usual funding sources, production facilities, and distribution avenues that are open to someone in her line of work: the

NFB, the CBC, Telefilm Canada, the Canada Council, BC Film, even Channel Four when that once illustrious British television station was still bankrolling new non-fiction features at the rate of one per week. The Film Board money behind *A Rustling of Leaves* was admittedly obtained by exceptionally "sneaky" means: the NFB parlayed a $5,000 development grant into over a quarter of a million dollars in hidden services because the federal government did not wish to look as if it were in cahoots with the Communist rebel army at the centre of her film.

What she has *not* done, however, is sacrifice her independence. Every one of the aforesaid films, made over a period of 18 years, is an essentially independent production. The only exception is her new, forty-five-minute "sequel" to *FIX*, "Bevel Up," (part of an interactive, multimedia DVD) which is unusually difficult to classify a) because it's her only *film à commande* and b) because, if you factor in the "topic" segments which she also shot, the end result is as long as her three shortest features.

Even more intriguingly, on the aesthetic level, her work tends to incorporate elements from every one of the earlier eras of documentary filmmaking. Wild's love of the everyday is easily the equal of that of Auguste Lumière, even if, as in *FIX*, the Downtown Eastside reality of Vancouver is represented by hypodermics stuck into telephone poles, and early morning rituals combine tooth brushing with shooting up. Conversely, she runs even more outdoor risks than Robert Flaherty, who, to the best of my knowledge, never lost a crew member to a round fired during the course of a jungle gun fight, which is precisely what happened to Wild during the making of *A Rustling of Leaves*; prioritizes progressive politics in a manner reminiscent of Dziga Vertov at his most optimistic (in other words, before he was effectively silenced by Stalin); respects Third World "talking heads" as profoundly as Jean Rouch while not shying away from Griersonian voice-over commentary; incorporates avant-garde elements from time-to-time (even if her model is more likely to be the Jean-Luc Godard of the late 1960s than the Man Ray of the mid 1920s); and pushes tiny crews with lightweight equipment into corners of the world where most *cinéma direct* advocates would fear to tread, however carefully.

As the director herself is the first to acknowledge, she is primarily a storyteller—with her background in theatre, radio and creative writing, it could hardly be otherwise—and every story requires characters. In documentary, of course, characters are found, not created, and Wild seemingly knows what she hopes to unearth before she even starts searching.

In Robert McKee's Manichean universe, storytelling implies the discovery of, and conflict between, protagonists and antagonists. The protagonists in Wild productions are generally flamboyant, charismatic Third World rebels of a photogenically Quixotic bent (Kummander Dante, Subcomandante Marcos...). She also has an obvious weakness for eloquent exponents of Liberation Theology, all of whom practice some form of Christianity (reactionary believers, conversely, are usually ranked among the villains). Antagonists, on the other hand, tend to be more fragmentary, a host of establishment voices in lieu of a single right-wing firebrand (the major exceptions to this rule being Jun Pala, the "anti-Communist" DJ in *A Rustling of Leaves*, and Bryce Rositich, the junkie-hating architect and motivating force behind the business-oriented Community Alliance in *FIX*). For someone with a strong sense of story structure, a quality this filmmaker obviously possesses in spades, such people would usually be described as "shadows of the antagonist," a strategy which, in this instance, abstracts the "enemy," turning him or her into U.S. Foreign Policy, international capitalism, or some other amorphous evil, a circumstance that should not be construed as a conscious editorial policy on the filmmaker's part, or as a will towards compiling court dockets that the objective evidence cannot support.

The previous paragraph should not, however, mislead the reader into believing that Wild specializes in agitprop cartoons. She does not. The journalistic integrity espoused by newspapers-of-record is always present in her motion pictures, even if this essential tool is never permitted to lull the viewer into a false sense of complacency. If characters often seem larger-than-life, there is nothing mythological about them. Like Cesare Zavattini, the spiritual godfather of Italian neorealism, Wild clearly believes that movies should be "about the real problems of real people living in the real world."[4] And like Jean Renoir, the most important exponent of poetic realism in the 1930s, Wild concurs with his period sentiment that "everyone has his reasons." Of course her films have narrative structure and political "bias"; that doesn't make them fraudulent, any more than it deprives them of a frequently breathtaking beauty.

Like Caspar David Friedrich and other nineteenth century Romantics, Wild is irresistibly drawn to remote mountain regions (the places that, according to *Annaliste* historian Fernand Braudel, are always the last to be brought under the control of centralized authority) and to the meanest streets of cities that are usually photographed only on their sunniest side (be they Vancouver or Manilla), which should perhaps be interpreted as some kind of dark, Baudelairean romanticism. The misty mountains and the teeming garbage dumps of the Philippines are emblematic of this bifurcated vision, as are the giant cedars and soulless office towers of the locally shot *Blockade*. The aforesaid dynamic is slightly different in *A Place Called Chiapas*, and even more so in *FIX*, where the natural world is not permitted to intrude in any way, shape or form, and beauty must manifest itself via the pathos of the human condition. To escape from the ugliness of the "underworld," one must testify to its horrors.

In this role, women witnesses are particularly important, although they're harder to classify according to Robert McKee's rather rigid formulae, generally being more down-to-earth than such Quixotic archetypes as Kummander Dante, Subcomandante Marcos, and Art Loring (the last of whom is the ex-logger and wing chief of the Eagle Clan of the Gitxsan nation, who fights for his people's right to develop their territory as they see fit in *Blockade*), although that certainly doesn't make them Sancho Panzas—they're as willing to tilt at windmills as the next hero. Still, it's sometimes hard *not* to think of many of Wild's female witnesses as "shadows of the protagonist" (except, obviously, in *Bevel Up*, where the heroes are all female public health nurses teaching junkies how to live more comfortably and safely with their intravenous addictions). It isn't difficult to tell which characters Wild warms to in her movies, even if the Devil is always allowed his say. Ironically, this bias is so upfront it makes the more subtly skewed emphases of the classical, "objective" documentary allegedly practised by network TV seem even more dishonest than it already does.

What this means, basically, is that Wild is aware of documentary tradition, but not enslaved by it. It also means she's as much of an auteur as any of her fictional counterparts, despite the extra work required to make the real world function like a studio set.

Let's consider some of the tropes she borrows from narrative cinema. The final moments of *Blockade*, for instance, are deliberately structured like a climactic "western shootout" (only this time the "Indians" get the better of the "cowboys". The scene also bears more than a passing resemblance to the denouement of *Matewan* [1987], John Sayles's fictional reconstruction of the Wobbly/hillbilly coal wars of the 1920s). Similarly, IBM-salesman-turned-junkie Dean Wilson's impossible love for kind-but-opaque, Christian, safe injection site activist Ann Livingston is not without its *Romeo and Juliet* poignancy. As for *A Place Called Chiapas*, its first five minutes are not unlike the opening moments of any taut political thriller (think vintage Costa-Gavras).

Occasionally, this same trick is played with certain documentary images that are universally accessible to the point of inescapability. Thus, when Ferdinand Marcos is evacuated by U.S. helicopter from the roof of his palace, everyone in the audience automatically recalls Uncle Sam's last humiliating moments in Vietnam a decade earlier.

This eclecticism is likewise reflected in her choice of crew. Wild's principal cinematographer has always been Kirk Tougas—out of necessity, she generally functions as her own second unit camera person—but she collaborates with a different editor on virtually every production (although apparently not from choice. "I would work with any one my editors again," the filmmaker insists, "but whenever it comes time to cut one of my films, they always seem to be involved in something else."). Certain people—Betsy Carson, Gary Marcuse, Sal Ferreras—have a role in most, if not all, of her motion pictures, although not always in the same role. How like the NFB in its unfettered past!

Whether to cut costs, to increase each feature's sense of personal authenticity, or just to get some extra mileage out of her early training as an actor, Wild is the narrator on all of her films that have narration. This is always a bit of a gamble, not because her voice is in any way defective but because it is often possible to get a famous performer to read a written text off-screen either dirt cheap or pro bono and thereby increase the film's widescreen marketability. With the audience's growing awareness of the various causes championed by their favourite celebrities, this trend has become almost the rule in recent years; if Michael Moore blithely ignores it, it's only because he's become a kind of "star" himself.

In one important respect, Wild has either been uncommonly prescient or formidably lucky (pick one). Despite the changes that have shaken the world's power structures over the past twenty years, none of her films have become dated in the least.

Even *A Rustling of Leaves*, a documentary in which communism and anti-communism contend for mastery in the Filipino countryside and capital, has not been rendered obsolete by the collapse of the Berlin Wall (despite the occasional onscreen presence of a functioning manual typewriter). This is because, in the Third World, socialism has not died the death assigned to it by Francis Fukuyama and America's other (past tense) neoconservatives. Indeed, in April of 2008, Evo Morales, Bolivia's first indigenous president, argued that, if the world is to survive, the capitalist system must be replaced by something more humane and viable. While the world's cameras—in many ways indistinguishable from the world's business press—remain focused on the so-called economic "miracles" of India and China, Latin America, in blithe defiance of the IMF and the World Bank, moves further and further to the left (even Mexico's last election was probably "hijacked" by U.S. money, to make sure the pro-NAFTA candidate could be seen supposedly steering the ship of state, someone like President Zedillo, one of the minor villains in *A Place Called Chiapas*).

Admittedly, the Philippines is an Asian, not a Latin American, country, but its long history as, first, a Spanish colony and, then, a U.S. dependency makes it at least an honorary member of that geographically unfortunate bloc. Even the local language is as indebted to the tongue of Cervantes as it is to the tongues of Shakespeare and Pramoedya Ananta Toer (Indonesia's Nobel literary laureate who never was). What we see in *A Rustling of Leaves: Inside the Philippine Revolution* reminds us more of FARC in Colombia than it does of any conflict long since consigned to the dustbin of history. (Before travelling to a region, this painstaking filmmaker and her handpicked staff of researchers explore its history, politics, sociology and economics very thoroughly. Ironically, Wild did *not* seem to pick up on the potential for

Islamic insurgency in Mindanao, the island where she did most of her filming for *A Rustling of Leaves*. Although, maybe she did. It is self-evident that so much material cannot be crammed into a film of less than two hours. I would, therefore, be most reluctant to rule out the possibility that somewhere in the director's archives lurks a sheaf of twenty-year old notes that would have skewed *Rustling* away from Mao and towards the local embodiment of Osama bin Laden. Knowing that she wanted to say more about the Philippines's earlier Huk Insurgency, but could not for reasons of space and documentary coherence, greatly magnifies this possibility.)

Wild's emphasis on research probably owes something to her days as a CBC freelance foreign correspondent, but it is counterpointed by an assumed air of naïveté. The filmmaker approaches each subject as if she'd just fallen off the turnip truck, and needs to learn everything from the ground up.

It is a good technique, although not entirely without risk. Like Claude Lanzmann and Marcel Ophüls, Wild is good at giving devils enough rope to hang themselves (as the Filipino disc jockey does when he expresses both his admiration for Hitler and his willingness—nay, his *eagerness*—to substitute gun for microphone.) As the director somewhat ruefully concedes, "When I was younger, I think I used to be fascinated by evil." Her attempts to talk to everyone in their own language invariably wins her brownie points and she seemingly never condescends to anyone (yet another application of Jean Renoir's previously mentioned mantram.) Policemen let her through checkpoints and peasants don't brush her off as just another gawking urbanite. Perhaps, on some deep level, they realize that this visitor acknowledges that, of all civilization's myriad and shameful exploitations, the exploitation of countryside by city is the oldest and least challenged. As Wild says of our own hinterland, "A huge part of my heart is in the North. I holiday there as well as film there."

On the other hand, this approach does not result in many one-on-ones with heads of state. Both Presidents Zedillo and Aquino are seen either in a long shot or stock footage. Occasionally, the absence of an overly visible *parti pris* has cost Wild credibility with left-wing power brokers as well. The falling out with Subcomandante Marcos is probably the most famous example of this unfortunate tendency.

In *A Place Called Chiapas*, Wild earns the rebel leader's wrath by asking what he was doing to protect poor supporters in an isolated region of the province. While there was very possibly nothing that Marcos could have done to alleviate such an unfortunate situation, this was clearly something he did not want to admit in the middle of an international press conference of almost Woodstockian exuberance. When Wild demanded to know why he was cutting off future contact, the Subcomandante grumbled, "You know why."

It would perhaps be instructive to compare Wild's experience with Marcos to that of Ignacio Ramonet, until very recently the editor-in-chief of *Le Monde diplomatique*. The author of many books on geopolitical subjects, Ramonet is internationally recognized as one of the leading opponents of both neo-liberalism and globalization. In 2001, he published a collection of conversations with the man entitled *Marcos: La Dignidad Rebelde*. This 77-page volume so impressed Fidel Castro, the Cuban leader agreed to do a similar volume with the Spanish-born journalist, a book that would be ten times longer than the first.[5] In *Fidel Castro: Biographie à deux voix*, Ramonet asked a number of "awkward" questions (about Cuba's treatment of homosexuals; about the nation's refusal to abolish the death penalty; etc.), but nothing that called the leader to account for past or present "crimes" he didn't wish to acknowledge, concede, or rebut. Ramonet was discreet, in other words, or diplomatic (right-wing Cubans in Miami, I'm sure, would scream, "No! Cowardly!"). Nevertheless, he landed the "big fish," just like

Nettie Wild and Mexican cinematographer Eduardo Herrera film Subcomandante Marcos, military commander of the Zapatistas, 1996. Photo Credit: Helene Bamberger.

the hero of *The Old Man and the Sea* (which was, of course, written in Batista-era Havana).[5]

Still, if Wild's approach in this instance must be judged a tactical failure, it is unquestionably a very honourable "defeat." That the filmmaker's sympathies are solidly with the left is beyond question. Her heart is with the Mayans in the mountains of Chiapas, and not with the "Castillians" on the balconies of Mexico City, even if this partiality once led the RCMP to rather ludicrously suspect that the filmmaker was covertly subsidizing the Filipino New People's Army!

Nevertheless, that doesn't mean she's anyone's patsy. For her, *Hardtalk* clearly isn't just the name of a popular program on BBC's World Service.

It also doesn't mean that she's going to prioritize ideology over fact.

Thus, in *Blockade*, the struggle presented is not just between the white and First Nations communities, but also between the "suits" in Vancouver and the long-established loggers in the "boonies" (the Hobenshields, being both local timber magnates and multi-generational inhabitants of Northern British Columbia, falling somewhere in between). Another struggle pits one clan of the Gitxsan nation against another, this territorial dispute seeming to have preceded the one between the original inhabitants of the area and various representatives of "the Crown" by many generations. And while Wild's hopes clearly reside in the First Nations activists (indeed, her camera seems to have a bit of a crush on Art Loring), loggers' voices are clearly heard, and those voices are very different from those of the senior managers selling stumpage rights to Japanese brokers in Vancouver (*Blockade* was produced *before* Canada's forestry industry was bought out by U.S. multinationals). Even more strikingly, she shows us an Ontario couple being dispossessed of their retirement home by tribal chiefs and elders, the worst fear of those who oppose scrapping Canada's long outdated and controversial Indian Act (and a technique not so very different from the one employed by Gillo Pontecorvo in *The Battle of Algiers* [1966], a pro-FLN docudrama in which the "terrorists" emerge as the good guys even though they are shown committing all the "unspeakable crimes" that their opponents habitually accuse them of committing).

Statistics also play a role in Wild's cinema. Thus, we learn that, during the early days of the Zapatista uprising in Southern Mexico, "People died on both sides. Some said 150…some said five hundred." This is about as far removed from the inflationary body counts of contemporary propaganda as it's possible to get. We are also told that 650 ranches were "liberated" by the rebels in Chiapas, and we get to hear the laments of a family that lost three of them (as well as see the plight of those indigenous campesinos who do not seem to have benefited from this long-delayed—and technically illegal—form of land distribution).

Images are equally informative. In *A Place Called Chiapas*, those at the top of the Mexican pecking order all seem to have "Hidalgo" faces, while those at the bottom look unchangeably Mayan. In a land where the cult of the *mestizo* (or mixed race citizen) is officially trumpeted from every secular pulpit, the ruling class (with the interesting exception of senior officers in the military) strongly resemble Cortes and his Conquistadores. That the number of indigenous Mexicans is consistently underestimated seems abundantly clear without this claim ever being verbalized explicitly.

It is interesting to note that indigenous cultures are at least tangentially attached to all four of Nettie Wild's features (assuming one thinks of the Philippines as an indigenous country from which the European colonialists have definitively departed, even on the genetic level). Indeed, they are front and centre in every film, with the notable exception of *FIX* (in which, sadly, they play a major role in the largely mute "chorus of the damned"). That she treats all of them not only respectfully but equally is as admirable as it is unusual. Why unusual? Because one of the rules of colonialism that has yet to be understood, never mind ratified, is that colonialist sympathies are always greater when extended to the victims of "foreign" culprits.

Thus, white Australians can shed a tear more easily for Newfoundland's annihilated Beothuk than they can for the Tasmanian aborigines that they exterminated themselves, in the same way that Canadians continue to believe, in the face of abundant evidence to the contrary, that their treatment of this nation's original inhabitants was infinitely more humane than America's more blatant genocide (we fought fewer wars, to be sure, but that was primarily because we had fewer "European" communities to protect, except in Eastern Canada in the sixteenth, seventeenth and eighteenth centuries, when our ferocity was no less than that of the "Thirteen Colonies"). Indeed, if New Zealand were permitted to settle Sweden's (Lapp) "native problem," and said Scandinavians were then encouraged to address the outstanding Maori grievances, justice for First Nations people would probably be here already. Unfortunately, myopia is a national malady, while 20/20 vision only works when political vision is painlessly "far sighted."

Nettie Wild is fully aware of this, and her cinema reflects these accurate perceptions.

III.

So are there any general rules that apply to *all* of this filmmaker's *oeuvre*?

If one were to extrapolate from the evidence presented, here are some of the conclusions one would have to reach:

1) All of Wild's films are neorealistic in the sense that "they deal with the real problems of real people living in the real world." Let's think of this as her Headlines Theatre inheritance.

2) To a greater or lesser degree, all are predicated on the conflict between the under-privileged and the over-privileged.

3) They are all structured like stories, not essays. This is hardly surprising, as Wild's academic training was primarily in the dramaturgical arts, and her first film collaboration (*Right to Fight for Affordable Housing*) cross-cut musical numbers from Headlines Theatre's most popular production, *Buy Buy Vancouver*, with documentary footage shot in the city of the same name. In 1985, *Under the Gun*, another Headlines Theatre dramatization, 50% of which was ostensibly set in America's most important former colony, led directly to this producer/actor's first solo documentary (most of her TV and radio

experience would likewise issue from this serendipitous first cause). *A Rustling of Leaves* emerged from an invitation to establish a popular theatre for the New People's Army in the Philippines (given the Lower Mainland's large expatriate Filipino population, this offer cannot really be said to have come out of…um…*left* field). For the record, Wild ceased to be directly involved with Headlines Theatre after 1984, but she sat on its board until 2007. Still, a background is a background. Nothing theatrical, therefore, should be considered alien to her.

4) Because of this fondness for "fictional" formats, her documentaries borrow freely from the language and memory banks of narrative cinema.

5) To keep this tendency in check, Wild invariably serves as her own narrator (my interpretation; the director might well interpret this strategy very differently).

6) This narration is almost completely devoid of autobiographical content, a technique which, consciously or not, pushes her nonfiction features as far away from the Ross McElwee school of diaristic filmmaking as it's possible to imagine.

7) While traditional documentary techniques are not eschewed (competing points of view, voice-over commentary, etc.), one is never left in any doubt as to how the filmmaker stands in regard to any social issue (in this respect, her films seem haunted by the ghost of Barbara Kopple's immensely influential 1977 Oscar-winner *Harlan County, U.S.A.*).

8) Part of this "traditionalism" includes statistics. Thus, we learn that precisely 18 demonstrators were killed in massacre "A" while 650 ranches were expropriated in uprising "B." Dates are likewise important (as every First Nations activist, struggling against the provisions of the so-called Indian Act, knows full well). Whatever else you might say about these films, they are definitely *not* ahistorical.

9) Although her films are not "re-cut" by her documentary subjects

in the way that Jean Rouch's later projects were, it is obvious that not misrepresenting the voiceless is one of the director's primary concerns (no one could treat oral history with greater respect than Wild does in *Blockade*). *Some* form of consultation is therefore a foregone conclusion.

10) "Talking heads" are spoken "to," not "at."

11) Whenever possible, said subjects are addressed in their own language.

12) Like Marcel Ophüls grilling Grossadmiral Dönitz in *The Memory of Justice* (1976), as an interviewer Wild has a gift for piercing the armour of hostile witnesses (although this technique sometimes backfires, as it does in the case of Subcommandante Marcos...but, then, he was supposed to be a *friendly* witness).

13) What is said is sometimes so much at odds with what is shown, the effect is close to Dadaism. This has a lot to do with the director's choice of editors. In Wild's own words, "I have always looked for really strong, dramatic editors, people who will hold my feet to the dramatic fire."

14) There is virtually always some form of indigenous presence on- or immediately off-screen (an awareness that is in the very air you breathe if you happen to have had the good fortune to grow up on Canada's West Coast).

15) Physical beauty and striking imagery are both enthusiastically espoused, but never pointless prettiness.

16) Editing is dynamic, not mechanical. This applies to sound as much as it does to image (where Sal Ferreras invariably provides the percussion). This dynamism is often dialectical, in at least a quasi-Marxist sense.

17) Music is used sparingly, and it's more likely to be diegetic than the non-diegetic. In either instance, however, it seems equally appropriate and organic (Wild professes to prefer sound-scapes to traditional musical scores, which explains why the composers she hires do not habitually work in the motion picture industry).

18) There is a profound awareness that the countryside is permanently at the mercy of the Big City (or, in the case of *FIX* and *Bevel Up*, of the Inner City at the mercy of the "Outer").

19) Christianity is never far away from the thoughts of Wild's protagonists. For her heroes it is a process of liberation and a means to bettering the lives of the poor; for her villains it is constricting and buttresses repression up-to-and-including the point of judicial murder.

20) Subcommandante Marcos is not Wild's only Quixotic protagonist—in the director's own words, "My heroes are always tilting at windmills"—although he is unquestionably the one who most looks the part (seen on horseback like a latterday knight errant, smoking a "*patriote*" pipe through his helmet-like balaclava, distributing copies of his favourite book, *Don Quixote*, to all and sundry). One sees signs of the "Knight of the Woeful Countenance" in Art Loring (*Blockade*), Kummander Dante (*A Rustling of Leaves*), Ann Livingston (*FIX*), the street nurses in *Bevel Up*, etc. Whether this would be so noticeable if Cervantes's masterpiece *hadn't* recently celebrated its quadracentennial is questionable, but it's also typical of another aspect of Wild's cinema, which is…

21) …luck. Whether through prescience or exceptionally intelligent research, this documentarist makes movies about issues that don't sputter out into oblivion. Of course, what's good for a filmmaker isn't necessarily good for the world. If Russia hadn't suffered so horribly in World War Two, *Alexander Nevsky* (1938) would have lost much of its power. Conversely, if nuclear conflict *had* erupted between the United States and the Soviet Union, *The Seventh Seal* (1956) would have to be considered the greatest film of all time (even though no one would be left alive on earth to confirm this opinion).

22) Wild is not afraid to show her heroes in an unflattering light. Thus, we learn that the New People's Army eventually decided to

execute the teenaged traitor "Batman." In a similar vein—if you'll excuse the unintentional pun—the otherwise extremely sympathetic junkie Dean Wilson, when remembering his days as a mandatory "Aryan Brother" in a U.S. penitentiary, says in a chillingly dead voice, "You hate niggers, you hate spicks...you have to be racist in there. Otherwise you die."

23) Occasionally, heroes who do not fit Wild's usual paradigm are permitted to occupy centre stage. This happens in *FIX*, when Philip Owen, one of Vancouver's stodgiest mayors ever, champions safe injection sites, and imposes his viewpoint on his own reluctant party (the expressions on the faces of these outmaneuvered NPA stalwarts are priceless) despite the fact that this principled position will ultimately cost him his place at the apex of the city's urban pyramid.

24) Wild knows how to surf the Zeitgeist. She is an independent filmmaker who makes frequent use of public funding and government facilities. Her rise occurred at almost exactly the same moment when the "in-house" documentaries began to disappear from the Canadian landscape (although many of her closest editor-collaborators were trained in that then cooling, now stone cold "hothouse"). She hasn't so much changed with the times as learned to find an inner thread that does not date...and stick with it.

It should be transparent by now that most of the above categorizations are those of the author, not of his subject. This is because, regardless of the number of leitmotifs that one reads (rightly or wrongly) into her work, Nettie Wild is a director who relies on both feeling and serendipity. The films that she eventually makes all pivot on subjects that she simply cannot ignore, set in places that she cannot resist, featuring "characters" who resonate in her own personal mythology. They find her, in other words, as much as she finds them.

This makes her not just a national treasure but a provincial one as well. Even when she works in foreign lands, the mists and beauties of

Canada's mysterious, ultimately unfathomable raincoast are manifestly present.

And if all documentary is in some sense a lie, *absolutely no one* tries harder to tell the truth.

———————————————

Notes

[1] *The Architecture of Doom*. Dir. Peter Cohen. First Run Features, 1989. Film.

[2] Sontag, S. "Fascinating Fascism." *The New York Review of Books* 22.1 6 Feb. 1975. Print.

[3] See P. Morris, *Embattled Shadows: A History of Canadian Cinema, 1895-1939*. Montreal: McGill-Queen's University Press, 1978. Print.

[4] It might be worth mentioning that, in 1981, the filmmaker co-founded Headlines Theatre with that reality-based troupe's current director, David Diamond. Their most popular production was entitled *Buy Buy Vancouver*, a drama about the Lower Mainland's housing crisis with obvious affinities to Italian Nobel laureate Dario Fo's *We won't Pay! We won't Pay!* Since Fo is Italy's theatrical answer to Zavattini—albeit with a dash of *commedia dell'arte* thrown in for good measure—this particular artistic debt is indisputable. [Editor's note: Quotations of Nettie Wild in this text, unless indicated otherwise, are taken either from the raw transcript of the interview for this volume or from personal conversations between the essayist and the filmmaker.]

[5] I'm referring to the French translation in this instance, because that version contains one more chapter than the Spanish original.

NETTIE WILD

FILMOGRAPHY/MULTIMEDIA

2007   *Bevel Up: Drugs, Users and Outreach Nursing*, 4.5 hour
interactive DVD designed around a 45 min documentary
Director; Co-Producer with Betsy Carson, Fiona Gold,
Juanita Maginley, et al.

2002   *FIX: The Story of an Addicted City*, 92 min
Director; Co-Cinematographer with Kirk Tougas;
Co-Producer with Betsy Carson, Gary Marcuse.

1998   *A Place Called Chiapas*, 92 min
Director; Co-Writer with Manfred Becker;
Co-Cinematographer with Kirk Tougas; Co-Producer with
Betsy Carson, Kirk Tougas.

1994   *Blockade*, 90 min
Director; Co-Producer with Betsy Carson, Christain
Bruyere, Gary Marcuse.

1988   *A Rustling of Leaves: Inside the Philippine Revolution*,
112 min
Director; Writer; Second Camera; Co-Producer with
Christopher James, Peter Wintonic.

1984   *Gifted Kids*, 24 min
Narrator.

1982   *Right to Fight*
       Director; Producer with Headlines Theatre; Actress.

1981   *A Time to Rise*, 40 min
       Sound Recordist.

1981   *Distant Islands*, 6 min
       Narrator.

RETROSPECTIVES

Pacific Cinémathèque (2010)
Hot Docs Documentary Festival (2003)
Cinematheque Ontario (1999)

BIBLIOGRAPHY

1985

Wild, Nettie. "5 Letters from the Revolution." CBC Radio. *Morningside.* 1985. Radio documentary. 1986

Wild, Nettie. "Boycott." CBC Radio. *Morningside.* 4 Feb. 1986. Radio documentary.

_____. "Peace Talks." CBC Radio. *Sunday Morning.* 10 August 1986. Radio documentary.

_____. "Commentary." CBC Radio. *Sunday Morning.* 30 Nov. 1986. Radio commentary.

1988

Aird, Elizabeth. "Wild Plunges into a Revolution." *The Georgia Straight* 4-11 Nov. 1988: 4. Print.

Lacey, Liam. "A Dynamic, Disturbing look at Revolution." *The Globe and Mail.* 17 Oct. 1988. C7. Print.

O'Neil, Mark. "Nettie Wild's *A Rustling of Leaves*: *Inside the Philippine Revolution.*" *Cinema Canada* 158 (December 1988): 29-30. Print.

Wild, Nettie. "Getting Aired: The 'Right' Spin." *Cinema Canada* 158 (December 1988): 17-18. Print.

1989

Barrett, Tom. "Lives on the Line." *Vancouver Sun* 5 May 1989: D1. Print.

Euvrard, Michel. "Entretien avec Nettie Wild." *24 Images* 46 (November/December 1989): 40-41. Print.

Griffen, John. "Nettie Wild: Hustle of Love is Working." *The (Montreal) Gazette*. 22 June 1989. Print.

Grugeau, Gérard. "*A Rustling of Leaves*: Inside the Philippine Revolution de Nettie Wild." *24 Images*. 46 (November-December 1989): 41. Print.

Johnson, Brian D. "Guerrillas in the Mist." *Maclean's* 102.17 24 April 1989: 63. Print.

Mahrenholz, Simone. "A Rustling of Leaves." *Der Tagespiegel.* 17 Feb. 1989. Print.

Petrowski, Nathalie. "La Revolution Vue de l'Interieur." *Le Devoir*. 21 Juin 1989. Print.

Petrowski, Nathalie. "Le documentaire comme guerilla." *Le Devoir*. 23 Juin 1989. Print.

Smith, Doug. "Shootout at the Reality Factory." *In These Times* 32. 30 Aug.– 5 Sept. Year Unknown. Print.

Taylor, Noel. "Heroes and villains in Philippines." *The Ottawa Citizen*. 25 April 1989. Print.

Wintonick, Peter. "Time, Trust and Money: Inside Stories about the Production of *A Rustling of Leaves*: Inside the Philippine Revolution." *Cinema Canada* 160 (February-March 1989): 13-16. Print.

1990

Bronstein, Phil. "A 'Rustling' of Revolution." *San Francisco Examiner* 14 May 1990: D1. Print.

Guevarra, Leslie. "Underground in Philippines." *San Francisco Chronicle*. 11 May 1990: E1. Print.

Thomas, Kevin. "Leaves Probes Philippine Revolution." *Los Angeles Times*. 24 May 1990. Print.

Merina, Victor. "Guerrillas in the Mist." *Los Angeles Times*. 16 May 1990. Print.

1991

Marcuse, Gary and Wild, Nettie. "Inside the Philippine Revolution." CBC Radio, *Ideas*. June 17, June 18, 1991. Radio documentary.

1993

McCullough, Michael. "Born Wild." *Vancouver Sun*. 9 Oct. 1993: D11. Print.

Posner, Michael. "Hanging on To The Horses: *A Rustling of Leaves*: Inside the Philippine Revolution." chap. in *Canadian Dreams: The Making and Marketing of Independent Films*. Vancouver-Toronto: Douglas & McIntyre, 1993. 51-78. Print.

Wood, Chris. "This Land is my Land." *Maclean's*. 29 Nov. 1993: 46. Print.

1998

Birnie, Peter. "Wild ride into rebel territory." *Vancouver Sun*. 16 Sept. 1998. C5. Print.

_____. "Beautifully Balanced Look at Mexico's Chiapas rebels." *Vancouver Sun*, 18 Sept. 1998. C3. Print.

Bissley, Jackie. "Film-Maker Nettie Wild Talks about Chiapas." *Windspeaker*. 16.6 Oct. 1998: 14. Print.

Costabile, J. Paul. "A Documentary in the Finest NFB Tradition" (Review of *A Place Called Chiapas*). *Catholic New Times* 22.18 (22 Nov. 1998): 17. Print.

Eisner, Ken. "Place Called Chiapas Aims at the Heart of Rebellion." *The Georgia Straight*. 17-24 Sept. 1998. Print.

Johnson, Brian D. "Masked Men and Disco Kings." *Maclean's* 111.38 (21 Sept. 1998): 77-78. Print.

Johnston, Andrew. "A Place Called Chiapas." *Time Out, New York*. Critics Pick. 5-12 Nov. 1998. Print.

Kllawans, Stuart. "Zapatista Realidad." *The Nation*. 23 Nov. 1998. Print

O'Connell, Clodagh. "The Passionate Eye." *Vancouver Courier*. No. 73. 13 Sept. 1998. Print.

Saunders, Doug. "The Camera's Unblinking Eye: Uprising in Chiapas." *Globe and Mail* (Toronto) 22 September 1998: A19. Print.

Stratton, David. "A Place Called Chiapas." *Variety*. 2-8 (March 1998): 88. Print.

Vermee, Jack. "The West Coast." *Take 1* 7.21 (Toronto) (Fall 1998): 42. Print.

1999

Holden, Stephen. "Examining Mexico's Zapatista Uprising." *New York Times*. 4 Nov 1998: 3. Print.

Morris, Wesley. "Exploring the Unexpected Facets of Chiapas." *San Francisco Examiner*. 11 June 1999. Print.

Stone, Judy. "A Revolutionary Eye." *San Francisco Examiner*. 10 June 1999. Print.

Wild, Nettie. "In Search of Light on the Road to Jolnixtie." *Brick* no. 63 (Fall 1999): 8-17. Print.

2000

Jeff T. Dick. "A Place Called Chiapas" (Review). *Library Journal* 125.17 (15 Oct 2000): 120. Print.

Johnston, Josée. "Pedagogical Guerrillas, Armed Democrats, and Revolutionary Counterpublics: Examining Paradox in the Zapatista Uprising in Chiapas Mexico." *Theory and Society* 29.4 (August 2000): 463-505.

Nichols, Peter M. "Getting to Know Outcast Cultures." *New York Times*. 13 Oct. 2000: 34. Print.

Wild, Nettie. "Untitled." *Point of View* no. 39 (Spring 2000): 11. Print.

2002

Beard, William and Jerry White (eds.). *North of Everything: English Canadian Cinema Since 1980.* Edmonton: University of Alberta Press, 2002. Print.

Gill, Alexandra. "The Mayor, the Addict and the Filmmaker" (Review of *FIX*). *Globe and Mail* (Toronto) 2 October 2002: R8. Print.

MacQueen, Ken. "Needles, Love and Revolution." *Maclean's* 115.46 (18 November 2002): 120. Print.

Monk, Katherine. "Wild's Look at Addicts' Lives Breaks

Stereotypes" (Review of *FIX*). *The Vancouver Sun* 14 September 2002. Print.

_____. "Wild's Ride with the Mayor." *The Vancouver Sun*. 16 Oct. 2002: B11. Print.

2003

Carnignan, Gilles. "*FIX*: un Junkie, un Maire, Un combat." *Le Soleil* (Quebec). 21 Nov. 2003: B8. Print.

Griffen, John. "Urban Decay." *The (Montreal) Gazette*. 7 Nov. 2003. Print.

_____. "*FIX* becomes part of the solution." *The (Montreal) Gazette*. 8 Nov. 2003. Print.

Groen, Rick. "Looking for an uneasy fix." *The Globe and Mail*. 17 Oct. 2003. Print.

Johnston, Josée and Gordon Laxer "Solidarity in the Age of Globalization: Lessons from the Anti-MAI and Zapatista Struggles" *Theory and Society* 32.1 (February 2003):39-91. Print.

Lacey, Liam. "It's a Wild Road Show." *The Globe and Mail* (Toronto) 16 Oct. 2003: R4. Print.

Lavoie, Andre. "La face cachee de Vancouver." *Le Devoir*. 9 Nov. 2003: E8. Print.

Lepage, Aleksik. "Vancouver a de la veine." *La Presse*. 8 Nov. 2003. Print.

Lyons, Tom. "A Passion for Social Justice: The Activist Films of Nettie Wild." *Take One* 11.41 (March-May 2003): 24-26. Print.

Onstad, Katrina. "Bringing Junkies to a cinema near you." Title Unknown. October 15, 2003. Print.

Pevere, Geoff. "Very human trio at heart of chronic drug storm." *Toronto Star*. 17 Oct. 2003. Print.

Reid, Michael. "Fixing a Problem." *Times Colonist*. 27 Feb. 2003. Print.

2005

Evers, Pamela. "A Place Called Chiapas" (DVD Review). *Film International* 18 (2005): 48. Print.

Feldman, Seth. "Canadian Social Documentary in the Age of Michael Moore: *The Corporation* and *FIX*." *CineAction!* 65 (January 2005): 17-19. Print.

2007

Smaill, B. "Injured Identities: Pain, Politics and Documentary." *Studies in Documentary Film* 1.2 (2007): 151-63. Print.

2008

Pablo, Carlito. "Intimate Lessons on Vancouver Streets." *The Georgia Straight*. 24 April 2008. Print.

"The POV Interview: Nettie Wild." Interviewed by Marc Glassman (Two-Part). *POV* 70-71 (Summer-Fall 2008): 5-11, 5-12. Print.

2009

Capturing Reality: The Art of Documentary. Dir. Pepita Ferrari. 101 Distribution, 2009. DVD.

Gold, Fiona. "Street Nursing." *American Journal of Nursing.* 109.7
(July 2009): 28-32. *LWW Journals.* Web. 3 Oct. 2009.

Nielsen, Lisa. "Nettie Wild: Changing Minds." *Citizenshift: Media
for Social Change.* National Film Board of Canada, 2009. Web.
7 Oct. 2009. <http://citizenshift.org/nettie-wild-changing-
minds>.

Contributor Notes

Mark Harris (critical essay) has a Master's degree in Film Studies and a Ph.D. in Comparative Literature, both from the University of British Columbia, the institution at which he currently teaches. A prize-winning playwright, Dr. Harris has approximately 4,000 articles in more than 50 periodicals in Canada and the U.S., although locally he is probably best known for his movie reviews in *The Georgia Straight*.

Claudia Medina (Interview) is a filmmaker, writer, and educator from the West Coast of BC. Her filmmaking deals with the stories and influences of her tri-national background (Mexico, Italy, Canada) and how they are transposed onto the Canadian cultural landscape. She also dedicates herself to filmmaking and facilitating youth to tell their own stories through this medium, and has developed curriculum and taught filmmaking workshops for many years now. She also works as a camera operator, editor, and field producer for documentaries and collaborates with artists of disciplines on performance/installation events in which she does live video mixing.

Brian Ganter (Series Editor) is a writer, educator, and filmmaker as well as an instructor at Capilano University in Vancouver. He has published in a variety of scholarly journals—from *Textual Practice* to *The Capilano Review*—and been an invited speaker and presenter at a variety of cinema studies and media studies conferences. In addition to a variety of shorts produced and screened in New York, where Brian resided for some time, he also co-directed the 2008 feature documentary *Metropole*, which has screened internationally in festivals and forums in Vancouver (Canada), Seattle (U.S.), and London (England). He is the former Media Literacy Coordinator in the Pacific Cinémathèque's Education Department, where he has continued to work on both present and future volumes of the PCP Monograph Series.